Multive

The True Nature O

The lifelong unraveling of the truth about reality and how we are Multiversal sentient beings currently having a human experience

By

T J Owen

Copyright ©2023 Trevor John Owen

Acknowledgements

Thanks to Guy Steven Needler for all his help, advice and guidance this book would not have ever been written without his wisdom and knowledge.

Contents

- First cracks in reality - page 3
- The clair senses – page 9
- Dreams and the Multiverse – page 10
- Seeking understanding – page 24
- Expansion of awareness of a wider reality – page 36
- Discovering who I really am – page 57
- Guy Needler and the structure of the Multiverse – page 66
- What are aliens? – page 73
- Three genres of alien vehicles – page 80
- Where Aliens come from – page 84
- A reason for abductions – page 87
- What are humans and how we incarnate – pg 91
- The structure whilst we incarnate – page 98
- How we incarnate – page 100
- How we incarnate affects us psychologically – page 107
- Diary of continuing experiences and understanding – page 111
- Pleiadians and other ET beings – page 122
- My analogy on the Multidimensionality of our existence – page 138
- Further reading – page 143

Multiverse – description:

The concept of multiple universes, or a multiverse, has been discussed throughout history, including Greek philosophy. It has evolved over time and has been debated in various fields, including cosmology, physics, and philosophy. Some physicists argue that the multiverse is a philosophical notion rather than a scientific hypothesis, as it cannot be empirically falsified. In recent years, there have been proponents and sceptics of multiverse theories within the physics community. Although some scientists have analyzed data in search of evidence for other universes, no statistically significant evidence has been found. Critics argue that the multiverse concept lacks testability and falsifiability, which are essential for scientific inquiry, and that it raises unresolved metaphysical issues.

Metaphysics – description:

Derived from the Greek meta ta physika ("after the things of nature"); referring to an idea, doctrine, or posited reality outside of human sense perception. In modern philosophical terminology, metaphysics refers to the studies of what cannot be reached through objective studies of material reality.

Metaphysics is considered one of the four main branches of philosophy, along with epistemology, logic, and ethics. It includes questions about the nature of consciousness and the relationship between mind and matter, between substance and attribute, and between potentiality and actuality.

First cracks in reality

In the year 1977, I was 12 years old and I saw, or rather had a 'close encounter' with a UFO, now called a UAP. Which in my humble opinion, is a continuing effort to obfuscate the admittance of beings that are here, but from 'other places' i.e. not Earth, and perhaps some are from the multiverse.

However, before I continue, let me first establish what is meant by a 'close encounter' or CE 1- 5, this is a rundown of the scale:

This terminology and the system of classification behind it was started by astronomer and UFO researcher J. Allen Hynek, and was first suggested in his 1972 book *The UFO Experience: A Scientific Inquiry*. He introduced the first three kinds of encounters; more sub-types of close encounters were later added by others, but these additional categories are not universally accepted by UFO researchers, mainly because they depart from the scientific rigor that Hynek aimed to bring to ufology.

Sightings more than 500 feet (160 m) from the witness are classified as "Daylight Discs," "Nocturnal Lights," or "Radar/Visual Reports." Sightings within about 500 feet are sub classified as various types of "close encounter." Hynek and others argued a claimed close encounter must occur within about 500 feet to greatly reduce or eliminate the possibility of misidentifying conventional aircraft or other known phenomena.

Hynek's scale achieved cachet with the general public when it informed elements of the 1977 film *Close Encounters of the Third Kind*, which is named after the third level of the scale. Posters for the film recited the three levels of the scale, and Hynek himself makes a cameo appearance near the end of the film.

Hyneks Scale:

First

A sighting of one or more unidentified flying objects:

- Flying saucers
- Odd lights
- Aerial objects that are not attributable to known human technology

Second

An observation of a UFO, and associated physical effects from the UFO, including:

- Heat or radiation
- Damage to terrain
- Crop Circles
- Human paralysis (Catalepsy)
- Frightened animals
- Interference with engines or TV or radio reception.
- Lost Time: a gap in one's memory associated with a UFO encounter.

Third

An observation of what Hynek termed "animate beings" observed in association with a UFO sighting. Hynek deliberately chose the somewhat vague term "animate beings" to describe beings associated with UFOs without making any unfounded assumptions regarding the beings' origins or nature. Hynek did not necessarily regard these beings as "extraterrestrials" or "aliens." Additionally, Hynek further expressed discomfort with such reports, but felt a scientific obligation to include them, at the very least because they represented a sizable minority of claimed UFO encounters.

Fourth

A human is abducted by a UFO or its occupants. This type was not included in Hynek's original close encounters scale.

Jacques Vallee, Hynek's erstwhile associate, argued that a CE4 should be described as "cases when witnesses experienced a transformation of their sense of reality," so as to also include non-abduction cases where absurd, hallucinatory or dreamlike events are associated with UFO encounters.

Fifth

Named by Steven M. Greer's CSETI group, these purported encounters are joint, bilateral contact events produced through the conscious, voluntary and proactive human-initiated or cooperative communication with extraterrestrial intelligence. This is very similar to some "contactees" of the 1950s who claimed regular communication with benevolent aliens.

While the nature of this bilateral communication is generally claimed to be telepathic, the experiencers in this group (as defined by CSETI) generally do not claim to be psychic if they should happen to think of themselves as contactees (in the strictest sense of the meaning of that terminology), insofar as contact, at least initially, is unilateral communication coming from the otherworldly intelligence to its subjects. Contrary to popular belief, not all experiencers in this group necessarily equate their communiqué as being with aliens.

With that said I go back to my 'sighting'. I lived in a small village called Normandy in Surrey in the South East of the UK. A friend had asked me to do his early morning paper round for him whilst he was on holiday for a week. You had to be 13 yrs old to do an early morning paper round, but as there was no-one else to do it in the quiet village the distributors allowed me to do it. One of these mornings I was cycling down Bailes lane, a dead end road with common land at the end which went for miles toward the nearest town of Guildford and had a couple of farms which were accessible by tracks from the end of the lane onto the common land. As I was cycling past the fields on the way to the end I felt something on my shoulder. I turned to look and there looking straight at me was a bird, a bird of prey no less, it looked like a Buzzard. I had the feeling that it was saying 'hello' to me. I said hello back in my mind and it then took off and flew away. That was a very strange occurrence, It left me with a nice feeling, but not as strange as what was about to confront me.

I turned the corner and was pedaling up a slight incline towards the end of the lane when ahead and to the right under the dark heavily laden cloud cover was a bright light. It was elliptical in shape and had very defined edges, despite the light emanating from it being extremely bright, brighter than any normal light (*close encounter of the first kind*). It was completely silent, and moving in a slow South Easterly direction towards Guildford. The idea of space and its inhabitants was of interest to me, I watched 'Dr Who' and 'UFO' and 'space 1999' with glee and excitement. I would imagine a spaceship coming down and the jolly spacemen inviting me aboard to see the ship and maybe even take me for a trip aboard.

But on seeing this ship of light in front of me, I stopped pedaling and became motionless. In fact I found that I was extremely scared and I was now unable to move any of my limbs (*Close encounter of the second kind – Human Paralysis or catalepsy*). I wanted to turn around and cycle home as fast as possible to get away, but I was frozen, like a rabbit caught in the headlights of a car. The ship slowly passed across in front of me, silently, it was perhaps 30 to 100 foot across, I wasn't sure as I couldn't judge the distance, maybe bigger? My head and eyes moved with the craft as it went across the sky; it was involuntary movement as the only thing I really wanted to move was my legs in furious pedalling! All the time as I could see the craft, in my head I was saying a mantra "Don't come near me, don't come near me, don't come near me, Go away, go away, go away" over and over again I would be saying this in my head as the ship passed silently in front of me. Now it was off to the left of me and the clouds had a few breaks in them, the craft went behind a cloud, came out, went behind another cloud, came out, and went behind another cloud, this last time it didn't come out. After a few seconds when I was sure that it had gone and didn't return, full use of my limbs became restored and I was able to cycle back home in a rush.

Back home, I rushed into the house and hid underneath the Dining room table, my mother coaxed me out and I told her what I had seen. One of my sisters was there and heard everything, but didn't believe a word, she said to my mother "oh he just doesn't want to do the paper round and is trying to get out of doing it". Also apparently I had been gone long enough to have already finished the round, which I found very confusing. I was too frightened to go back out again and so my mother helped with the paper round that day. After this I now learned to keep quiet, not to mention things of that nature to anyone as people didn't believe it. But I was shown something extraordinary that day, that the world was a place where things were possible, things that even science and education say don't exist. But there it was, plain as day flying through the sky, so what else is possible? What else really exists?

In UFO lore sometimes people have 'screen memories' either implanted or their minds create a false memory to cover what they actually saw, as the reality is too much for the conscious mind to cope with. It seems popular for people to have dreamt about or remember seeing an owl when in fact it was an alien visitation. In this case I saw a bird of prey that landed on my shoulder, a very unlikely scenario in reality, it was in fact more likely to be a cover memory for something far more interesting, a *close encounter of the third and fourth kind*.

This is not the full story of this event, more is to be revealed to me in years to come, this was just to crack my mind and consciousness wide open, the first step in the unraveling of truth.

A sketch I drew of my 1977 encounter of the UFO

This experience was the beginning of a chain of other 'paranormal' experiences and further 'weirdness' in my life. It was indeed, I believe, a catalyst for my perceived 'reality' to start to crack wider open, and let more of the truth of the wider reality bleed in.

The Clair senses

I think at this point it is a good time to look at, and explain what the Clair senses are, and I will point out how some of my experiences relate to some of these as we go along.

1. **Clairvoyance** (clear seeing) you receive pictures in the form of images in your mind's eye. They may be vivid dreams, visions, mental images, or mini movies. You may be able to see colours of auras etc images may be literal or metaphorical.

2. **Clairaudience** (clear hearing) you are able to hear voices or messages from the spiritual realm.
3. **Claircognizance** (clear knowing) this is experiencing a knowing, a gut feeling in which you know to be true in your mind's eye, even though you did not see or hear it. It could be an insight or even a 'download'.
4. **Clairsentience** (clear physical feeling) this is where you actually feel the physical feeling in your own body of what someone else is experiencing and feeling in their body.

Dreams and the multiverse

Lucid Dreaming

What is Lucid dreaming?

In the psychology subfield of oneirology (the scientific approach to understanding dreams in relation to the functions of the brain), a **lucid dream** is a type of dream in which the dreamer becomes aware that they are dreaming while they are dreaming. It is a trainable skill. During a lucid dream, the dreamer may gain some amount of control over the dream characters, narrative, or environment, although this control of dream content is not the salient feature of lucid dreaming. Lucid dreaming has been studied and reported for many years. Prominent figures from ancient to modern times have been fascinated by lucid dreams and have sought ways to better understand their causes and purpose.

Many different theories have emerged as a result of scientific research on the subject and have even been shown in pop culture. Further developments in psychological research have pointed to ways in which this form of dreaming may be utilized as a form of sleep therapy.

The term *lucid dream* was coined by Dutch author and psychiatrist Frederik van Eeden in his 1913 article *A Study of Dreams*, though descriptions of dreamers being aware that they are dreaming predate the article. Van Eeden studied his own dreams between January 20, 1898, and December 26, 1912, recording the ones he deemed most important in a dream diary. 352 of these dreams are categorized as lucid.

Van Eeden created names for seven different types of dreams he experienced based on the data he collected:

- Initial dreams
- Pathological dreams
- Ordinary dreams
- Vivid dreams
- Demoniacal dreams
- General dream-sensations
- Lucid dreams

He said the seventh type, lucid dreaming, is "the most interesting and worthy of the most careful observation and study."

Definition

Paul Tholey laid the epistemological basis for the research of lucid dreams, proposing seven different conditions of clarity that a dream must fulfill in order to be defined as a lucid dream:

1. Awareness of the dream state (orientation)
2. Awareness of the capacity to make decisions
3. Awareness of memory functions
4. Awareness of self
5. Awareness of the dream environment
6. Awareness of the meaning of the dream
7. Awareness of concentration and focus (the subjective clarity of that state)

Later, in 1992, a study by Deirdre Barrett examined whether lucid dreams contained four "corollaries" of lucidity:

- The dreamer is aware that they are dreaming

- They are aware actions will not carry over after waking
- Physical laws need not apply in the dream
- The dreamer has a clear memory of the waking world

Barrett found less than a quarter of lucidity accounts exhibited all four.

Ancient

The practice of lucid dreaming, as in cultivating the dreamer's ability to be aware that they are dreaming, is central to both the ancient Indian Hindu practice of Yoga nidra and the Tibetan Buddhist practice of dream Yoga. The cultivation of such awareness was a common practice among early Buddhists.

Early references to the phenomenon are also found in ancient Greek writing. For example, the philosopher Aristotle wrote: "often when one is asleep, there is something in consciousness which declares that what then presents itself is but a dream." Meanwhile, the physician Galen of Pergamon used lucid dreams as a form of therapy. In addition, a letter written by Saint Augustine of Hippo in AD 415 tells the story of a dreamer, Doctor Gennadius, and refers to lucid dreaming.

My Lucid Dream experience (one of many)

I became interested in the waking and dreaming world, I pondered on how your consciousness went from waking consciousness to sleeping consciousness. How did you cross over, where was the point of no return, just how does it work? So I set about trying to find out. It's a practical experiment and not an easy one to complete. It basically comprises of watching yourself fall asleep and trying to notice at what point you go into sleep. I watched myself, and watching yourself falling asleep almost guarantees that you won't sleep, because it's a foreign concept to your mind. Normally you let go and think of something nice and then drift away into sleep. So for a few nights I couldn't sleep at all, and then for a few nights eventually through sheer tiredness fell asleep without notice. But eventually I got the practice just right. When I was very tired and the mind really needed the sleep, I would notice that the dots of white light that I could see on the back of my eyelids would begin to move around and form vague shapes. Then these shapes would become pictures and then as I got interested in the pictures I would follow them, and following these pictures took me into sleep. That's it! I exclaimed to myself, that's how it's done! You see pictures and get involved in them and follow them into sleep. Great but hang on what's going on now? Suddenly I realized that I was sleeping, but, was conscious of being asleep. So I started to take advantage of this and tried to make happen in my dreams what I wanted. This is fantastic, a playground for the mind. Interesting as it was it made sleeping a whole lot of fun. I would go to my bedroom in the middle of the afternoon just so I could lay down and go into conscious sleep or as we know it 'Lucid dreaming'. One time I thought about space and the depths of the universe, I was interested in the size and breadth of space and so tried to imagine it in my mind. I thought of where I was lying on my bed and kind of 'zoomed' out like a telephoto lens that was on full zoom but now retracting back. So I zoomed out to see the village, then further to see the county from the air, ok, now further to see the planet. Now it gets interesting to try and imagine the all the planets and the universe. Then all of a sudden it was completely black! And then a feeling came of standing on the edge of infinity. My breath was sucked away and I felt like I was on the edge of something so vast that I would be sucked in forever and never get out. This was my first spiritual experience, the feeling of infinity an experience rarely met, perhaps only by the most austere contemplatives in the depths of meditation. I wasn't ready for such an experience at such a young age, I pulled myself back into normal consciousness and took a deep breath, I didn't fancy doing that again.

Precognitive Dreams

Precognitive dreams are the most widely reported occurrences of precognition. Usually, a dream or vision can only be identified as precognitive after the putative event has taken place. When such an event occurs after a dream, it is said to have "broken the dream".

According to the Book of Genesis, God granted Joseph precognition through prophetic dreams and the ability to interpret the dreams of others.

In Judaism it is believed that dreams are mostly insignificant while others "have the potential to contain prophetic messages".

Hinduism has a subsystem of psychology called Indian psychology with dreams believed to contain information about the future. There are seven classifications of dream or 'swapna', in which those which become 'manifest' are called 'bhāvita'.

Precognition has a role in Buddhism with dreams believed to be 'mind-created phenomena'. Those dreams which 'warn of impending danger or even prepare us for overwhelming good news" are considered the most important.

Throughout history it has been believed that certain individuals have precognitive abilities, or that certain practices can induce such experiences, and these visions have sometimes been associated with important historical events. Despite the apparent lack of scientific evidence, many people still believe in precognition. A poll in 2005 showed 73% of Americans believe in at least one type of paranormal experience, with 41% believing in extrasensory perception.

Since ancient times precognition has been associated with dreams and trance states as well as waking premonitions, giving rise to acts of prophecy and fortune telling. Oracles, originally seen as sources of wisdom, became progressively associated with previsions of the future.

My precognitive experiences

A developed dream world led to these precognitive dreams, I also sometimes dreamt of my future life in allegorical terms rather than literal visions of what exactly would happen. The path of my life is normally represented by pathways and tracks in the countryside. I saw who I believed was my future wife down one of these tracks. A lady shorter than me, all I could see was long black hair, her head drooped downwards so her face could not be seen. I passed her and thought 'oh she looks sad' and went back to talk to her, waking before the conversation started. Indeed my future wife was Asian with long black hear and of a small stature, and indeed after meeting her I left, but went back and eventually married her. Another of these 'life' dreams involved me running down the tracks and across fields, trying to escape something unseen. I eventually hid behind a hedge thinking I was really well hidden, but the 'something' in pursuit knew exactly where I was and came straight to where I was hiding. What this represented is open to interpretation, but I was left with a feeling that there literally is 'Nowhere to hide' and that I can be found no matter what I did or where I went. I always associated this with an 'ET' presence, the 'watchers' as I always thought of them.

One of my dreams was very exact, I was walking down a path near my home when I was a teenager, I was maybe 14yrs old, I had something in my hand that I looked at with a glance, but couldn't tell what it was. Then I looked up quickly and a bus came along the road, stopped at the bus stop not far in front of me and some people got out. Then the dream ended, I forgot all about the dream as it seemed inconsequential at the time. But one day maybe a few days or a week later an old friend was visiting, who was living in the US but came with some toys, one was a pair of 'walkie-talkies', which were not available as such in the UK at that time. So I was very proud to be having one as I walked along the road with my friend just behind. I looked down glancing admirably at the walkie-talkie, then all of sudden I recognized the moment. It was like the dream I had before. I looked up suddenly to see the bus, yes, there it was! Coming along the road just as I had seen, then it stopped and some people got off, all exactly the same as my dream. That was where the dream ended. I turned and shouted excitedly "I have seen this, in a dream, exactly this!" my friend looked a little taken aback, but actually accepted something must have happened by the excitement I was in. It may at first seem like nothing in particular, but it was the beginning of me trying to shut off the many experiences that were to keep pouring into my life. I thought about this incident during the following days and weeks, and realised that what I saw, happened in my dream, through my own eyes, *exactly* as it had happened in reality. The same bus, the quickness I looked up (but only because I had seen it already, and in the dream I had *also* seen it already!) and all the cars, my friend, the way I held the walkie-talkie, the people on the bus, *all* of them, destined to be there at exactly that time, in exactly those places, wearing the same clothes doing the same things. *How* could this be possible? Does that mean we have no choice? Are we all destined to do the things we do, and we can't change it? And again, something else that is supposedly *not possible*, but here it is, a reality, but denied by all those we look up to as the holders of truth, the governments, the Politian's, the education system and the all knowing scientists. Who *can* you trust, it seemed everyone was lying and at the same time denying the very experiences I was having UFO's, ET's, seeing the future? Just what *is* possible?

Meaningful Dreams

I had another 'path of life' dream, but this time I was in a building, following corridors and taking which direction I felt was best, when eventually I came across a booth to the left, in it was a young lady, it had a kind of cut out in the glass for speaking, rather like in modern banks. Just past it to the right was a room, which looked like a gymnasium of sorts. It was maybe 20ft square, and had a climbing frame to the right and to the left was like a viewing room, with glass panels so that people could see into the room, but the entrance to the viewing room came from outside the building, which feels rather like 'outside of life' in a way. There was a door leading into the gym from the passageway I was in and on the far wall of the gym was a large archway maybe 10ft across which went into complete darkness. I was fascinated by this room and asked the lady what it was for. I also asked should I carry on or go into the room. She shrugged and said "up to you" and that was all she would say.

I couldn't resist it, and entered the room. I looked around and looked through the windows to see people going about their business outside, which I found quite strange as there isn't normally anyone in these kinds of dreams except myself or people directly related to my life. It was definitely one of those 'vivid life' kinds of dreams as it had a kind of realism and feel to it that was different to normal dreams. Then people started to enter the 'Viewing room' off to the left. It was all kind of irregular, I didn't recognize any of these people and I could see their faces quite clearly. They also had a very strange kind of look to them, they were emotionless and straight faced. They sauntered into the viewing room and just watched, silently.

So I looked at the climbing apparatus and thought "this is strange. What's it for?" I climbed up a bit then got off again. Ok, so now the dark exit to the back of the room was taking my attention and I started to walk towards it. As I neared the archway I noticed that the floor curved slightly to the left the other side of the archway and then went down quite steeply into the darkness below. As I went into the darkness I suddenly felt a bit scared, and then I didn't know how, but I *knew* that this was a representation of going down into my own mind or consciousness, the darkness of the unknown part of my unconscious mind, and now I think, also memories of understanding and lives gone before, which will make more sense later in the book. I walked slowly and was feeling rather scared when all of a sudden I heard a noise, then I looked and something was coming up out of the darkness towards me. It wasn't small either! I saw some very large legs and then decided that to turn and run for it was the best option. So I ran out of the tunnel and back into the gym, I saw the climbing frame and thought I should climb up it to get away and hopefully out of reach of the beast coming up.

I climbed the climbing fame and looked down in scared anticipation, and out of the darkness came the most enormous spider I have ever seen, monstrous in size! Itself maybe 7 or 8 feet across, and standing another 7 foot high. But there was something very different about this spider, it had a head, a *human* head and torso. It had the head and torso of a female. The large half human half spider stopped and didn't even attempt to climb the frame after me, she just stopped and looked at me and said *"you don't want to go down there, it's dangerous"* it was more of a friendly warning than a threat, there was no malice or threatening behavior from this being, then she wandered back through the archway and down into the darkness once more. I recovered from the experience reasonably quickly and felt that even though she seemed quite friendly, I didn't really want to come across her again. But there was an even bigger curiosity now with the dark recess of my mind, and I climbed down and stepped carefully back into the darkness of the descending tunnel. I paused momentarily in the darkness waiting for the steps of the large spider to return, ready to turn and run back to the climbing frame. But the spider did not return and with my heart pumping harder I stepped more into the darkness, what happened next I don't know, as the next thing I knew I was awake in the morning.

I think most, if not all of these Dream states of, precognitive, lucid and meaningful, come under the banner also of *Clairvoyance* as mentioned above.

Below is from " by Kavi B July 2021 in https://medium.com"

Dreams have long fascinated humanity, serving as a gateway to explore the unknown and unravel the mysteries of the mind. In recent years, the phenomenon of lucid dreaming has gained significant attention, allowing individuals to become aware within their dreams and exert control over their dreamscapes. This article delves into the intriguing connection between dreams, lucid dreaming, and the possibility of accessing other dimensions. By exploring various theories and scientific studies, we aim to shed light on this enigmatic realm of human consciousness.

The Nature of Dreams

Dreams are a natural occurrence that takes place during our sleep. They are a culmination of our thoughts, memories, emotions, and experiences, blending together to create vivid and sometimes bizarre scenarios. Throughout history, dreams have been seen as a source of inspiration, guidance, and prophetic visions.

Lucid Dreaming: The Gateway to Consciousness

Lucid dreaming is a phenomenon where individuals become aware that they are dreaming while still within the dream state. This heightened state of consciousness allows dreamers to actively participate in and manipulate their dreams. During lucid dreams, individuals can control their actions, alter the dream environment, and even interact with dream characters.

The Link between Dreams and Parallel Realities

Some theories suggest that dreams may provide glimpses into parallel realities or alternate dimensions. These dimensions may exist simultaneously alongside our own, yet remain hidden to our waking consciousness. Lucid dreaming, with its ability to access and control dreams, offers a potential pathway to explore and interact with these parallel realities.

Scientific Studies and Evidence

While the concept of accessing other dimensions through dreams may seem fantastical, several scientific studies have sought to investigate this possibility. One such study conducted by Dr. Stephen LaBerge at Stanford University explored the similarities between lucid dreaming and out-of-body experiences (OBEs). Participants who reported having OBEs during their dreams displayed striking similarities to those who experienced lucid dreams, suggesting a potential link between the two phenomena.

Additionally, research conducted by Dr. Ursula Voss and her team at Goethe University Frankfurt utilized electroencephalography (EEG) to analyze brain activity during lucid dreaming. The study found that certain brainwave patterns observed during lucid dreaming were similar to those seen in waking consciousness, further supporting the idea that lucid dreaming involves a heightened state of awareness and potential access to other dimensions.

The Multiverse Hypothesis

One intriguing concept that aligns with the idea of accessing other dimensions through dreams is the multiverse hypothesis. This hypothesis proposes that our universe is just one of many parallel universes, each with its own set of physical laws and possibilities. If this theory holds true, it suggests that dreams and lucid dreaming may provide windows into these alternate realities.

Practical Applications and Potential Implications

The exploration of dreams, lucid dreaming, and accessing other dimensions holds immense potential for various fields. From psychology and neuroscience to spirituality and metaphysics, understanding the connection between dreams and parallel realities could revolutionize our understanding of consciousness and the nature of reality itself.

Conclusion

While the connection between dreams, lucid dreaming, and accessing other dimensions remains a subject of ongoing investigation, the evidence and theories presented in this article highlight the tantalizing possibilities that lie within the realm of human consciousness. Whether dreams are mere figments of the imagination or gateways to parallel realities, one thing is certain: the study of dreams continues to captivate our curiosity and push the boundaries of our understanding. As we delve deeper into the mysteries of the mind, we may yet unravel the secrets hidden within the enigmatic realm of dreams and parallel realities.

Below is from *"By Michio Kaku. Dr Kaku is an American theoretical physicist, activist, futurologist, and popular-science writer. He is a professor of theoretical physics in the City College of New York and CUNY Graduate Center. June 20, 2022"*

This essay is part of a series called The Big Ideas, in which writers respond to a single question: What is reality

When I was 8 years old, a revelation forever changed my life.

The year was 1955, and newspaper headlines announced the death of a renowned scientist. A photo accompanied one article, showing his office desk strewn with papers and books. As I recall, the photo caption noted that among the stacks of material was an unfinished manuscript.

I was captivated by this discovery. What could be so challenging that this man, often hailed as one of the greatest scientists of all time, could not complete this work? I had to find out, and over the years I visited libraries to learn more about him.

His name was Albert Einstein. His unfinished work explored what would be known as the theory of everything, an equation, perhaps no more than an inch long, that would allow us to unify all the laws of physics. It would, as Einstein had hoped, give us a glimpse into the mind of God. "I want to know his thoughts," he famously said. I was hooked.

Today, many of the world's top physicists are embarking on this cosmic quest, whose far-reaching reverberations span our understanding of reality and the meaning of existence. It would be the crowning achievement of thousands of years of scientific investigation, since ancient civilizations also wondered how the universe was created and what it is made of. The ultimate goal of the theory of everything is to combine Einstein's theory of relativity with the bizarre world of quantum theory.

In essence, the theory of relativity delves into the cosmos's most massive phenomena: things like black holes and the birth of the universe. The domain of relativity is nothing less than the entire cosmos. Quantum theory, on the other hand, explores the behavior of matter on the most minuscule level. Its domain encompasses the tiniest particles of nature, those hidden deep inside the atom.

Unifying these two spheres of thought into a single and coherent theory is an ambitious undertaking, one that builds on and adds to the work that Einstein began. But to do this, scientists must first determine a crucial truth: where the universe came from.

This is where our two spheres of thought pointedly diverge.

If we subscribe to Einstein's relativity theory, the universe is a bubble of some sort that is expanding. We live on the skin of this bubble, and it exploded 13.8 billion years ago, giving us the Big Bang. This birthed the singular cosmos as we know it.

Quantum theory is based on a radically different picture — one of multiplicity. Subatomic particles, you see, can exist simultaneously in multiple states. Take the electron, a subatomic particle that carries a negative charge. Wondrous devices in our lives, such as transistors, computers and lasers, are all possible because the electron, in some sense, can be in several places at the same time. Its behaviour defies our conventional understanding of reality.

Here is the key: In the same way that quantum theory forces us to introduce multiple electrons simultaneously, applying that theory to the entire universe makes us have to introduce multiple universes — a multiverse of universes. By that logic, the solitary bubble introduced by Einstein now becomes a bubble bath of parallel universes, constantly splitting in two or bumping into other bubbles. In this scenario, a Big Bang could perpetually happen in distant regions, representing the collision or merging of these bubble universes.

In physics, the concept of a multiverse is a key element of a leading area of study based on the theory of everything. It's called string theory, which is the focus of my research. In this picture, subatomic particles are just different notes on a tiny, vibrating string, which explains why we have so many of them. Each string vibration, or resonance, corresponds to a distinct particle. The harmonies of the string correspond to the laws of physics. The melodies of the string explain chemistry.

By this thinking, the universe is a symphony of strings. String theory, in turn, posits an infinite number of parallel universes, of which our universe is just one."

Blue Brain Team Discovers a Multi-Dimensional Universe in Brain Networks

"Using mathematics in a novel way in neuroscience, the Blue Brain Project shows that the brain operates on many dimensions, not just the three dimensions that we are accustomed to For most people, it is a stretch of the imagination to understand the world in four dimensions but a new study has discovered structures in the brain with up to eleven dimensions – ground-breaking work that is beginning to reveal the brain's deepest architectural secrets.

Using algebraic topology in a way that it has never been used before in neuroscience, a team from the Blue Brain Project has uncovered a universe of multi-dimensional geometrical structures and spaces within the networks of the brain.

The research, published today in *Frontiers in Computational Neuroscience,* shows that these structures arise when a group of neurons forms a *clique*: each neuron connects to every other neuron in the group in a very specific way that generates a precise geometric object. The more neurons there are in a *clique*, the higher the dimension of the geometric object "We found a world that we had never imagined," says neuroscientist Henry Markram, director of Blue Brain Project and professor at the EPFL in Lausanne, Switzerland, and co-founder and Editor-in-Chief of Frontiers, "there are tens of millions of these objects even in a small speck of the brain, up through seven dimensions. In some networks, we even found structures with up to eleven dimensions."

Markram suggests this may explain why it has been so hard to understand the brain. "The mathematics usually applied to study networks cannot detect the high-dimensional structures and spaces that we now see clearly."

If 4D worlds stretch our imagination, worlds with 5, 6 or more dimensions are too complex for most of us to comprehend. This is where algebraic topology comes in: a branch of mathematics that can describe systems with any number of dimensions. The mathematicians who brought algebraic topology to the study of brain networks in the Blue Brain Project were Kathryn Hess from EPFL and Ran Levi from Aberdeen University."

(Posted on June 12, 2017 by Frontiers Communications in Neuroscience, https://blog.frontiersin.org)

Seeking Understanding

" *Guy*: Tell me then, why are we, those that are on the spiritual path, that is, allowed to think of ourselves as individuals, or individualized units of source?

Origin: Because it helps you to go in the right direction. You have to be fed the ultimate knowledge slowly, exposure to expansion only being possible when one displays the capability for expansion and not before, for that would be detrimental and creates regression."

(Guy Steven Needler - The Origin speaks, chapter 12 – what we really are, page 193)

Searching for a path

I needed to find answers to what all of my experiences meant, about life, the universe and everything. What did it all mean? Where do I go to find these answers?

I looked at science, but although things got very interesting at the quantum level, it didn't hold any answers. I then looked at esoteric philosophy, I read a few P.D. Ouspensky books, and they were very interesting even having some 'practical' practices to follow to achieve some states of mind, all very interesting, but again felt limited and didn't answer the specific questions of my personal experiences. I turned to philosophy, reading Plato's Republic, which contains his analogy of the cave, which is a must read. In fact I will put it here below for you to read and digest.

PLATO - The Allegory of the Cave - Translated by Shawn Eyer

Plato's famous allegory of the cave, written around 380 bce, is one of the most important and influential passages of The Republic. It vividly illustrates the concept of Idealism as it was taught in the Platonic

Academy, and provides a metaphor which philosophers have used for millennia to help us overcome superficiality and materialism. In this dialogue, Socrates (the main speaker) explains to Plato's brother,Glaukon, that we all resemble captives who are chained deep within a cavern, who do not yet realize that there is more to reality than the shadows they see against the wall.

Socrates: And now allow me to draw a comparison in order to understand the effect of learning (or the lack thereof) upon our nature. Imagine that there are people living in a cave deep underground. The cavern has a mouth that opens to the light above, and a passage exists from this all the way down to the people. They have lived here from infancy, with their legs and necks bound in chains. They cannot move. All they can do is stare directly forward, as the chains stop them from turning their heads around. Imagine that far above and behind them blazes a great fire. Between this fire and the captives, a low partition is erected along a path, something like puppeteers use to conceal themselves during their shows.

Glaukon: I can picture it.

Socrates: Look and you will also see other people carrying objects back and forth along the partition, things of every kind: images of people and animals, carved in stone and wood and other materials. Some of these other people speak, while others remain silent.

Glaukon: A bizarre situation for some unusual captives.

Socrates: So we are! Now, tell me if you suppose it's possible that these captives ever saw anything of themselves or one another, other than the shadows flitting across the cavern wall before them?

Glaukon: Certainly not, for they are restrained, all their lives, with their heads facing forward only.

Socrates: And that would be just as true for the objects moving to and fro behind them?

Glaukon: Certainly.

Socrates: Now, if they could speak, would you say that these captives would imagine that the names they gave to the things they were able to see applied to real things?

Glaukon: It would have to be so.

Socrates: And if a sound reverberated through their cavern from one of those others passing behind the partition, do you suppose that the captives would think anything but the passing shadow was what really made the sound?

Glaukon: No, by Zeus.

Socrates: Then, undoubtedly, such captives would consider the truth to be nothing but the shadows of the carved objects.

Glaukon: Most certainly.

Socrates: Look again, and think about what would happen if they were released from these chains and these misconceptions. Imagine one of them is set free from his shackles and immediately made to stand up and bend his neck around, to take steps, to gaze up toward the fire. And all of this was painful, and the glare from the light made him unable to see the objects that cast the shadows he once beheld. What do you think his reaction would be if someone informed him that everything he had formerly known was illusion and delusion, but that now he was a few steps closer to reality, oriented now toward things that were more authentic, and able to see more truly? And, even further, if one would direct his attention to the artificial figures passing to and fro and ask him what their names are, would this man not be at a loss to do so? Would he, rather, believe that the shadows he formerly knew were more real than the objects now being shown to him?

Glaukon: Much more real.

Socrates: Now, if he was forced to look directly at the firelight, wouldn't his eyes be pained? Wouldn't he turn away and run back to those things which he normally perceived and understand them as more defined and clearer than the things now being brought to his attention?

Glaukon: That's right.

Socrates: Now, let's say that he is forcibly dragged up the steep climb out of the cavern, and firmly held until finally he stands in the light of the sun. Don't you think that he would be agitated and even begin to complain? Under that light, would his eyes not be nearly blinded, unable to discern any of those things that we ourselves call real?

Glaukon: No, he wouldn't see them at first.

Socrates: It would take time, I suppose, for him to get used to seeing higher things. In the beginning, he might only trace the shadows. Then, reflections of people and other things in the water. Next he would come to see the things themselves. Then he would behold the heavenly bodies, and the heaven itself by night, seeing the light of the stars and the moon with greater ease than the sun and its light by day.

Glaukon: Indeed so.

Socrates: And then, I think, he would at last be able to gaze upon the sun itself—neither as reflected in water, nor as a phantom image in some other place, but in its own place as it really is.

Glaukon: Undeniably.

Socrates: And now, he will begin to reason. He will find that the sun is the source for the seasons and the years, and governor of every visible thing, and is ultimately the origin of everything previously known.

Glaukon: Of course. First he would see and then draw conclusions.

Socrates: That being the case, should he remember his fellow prisoners and their original dwelling and what was accepted as wisdom in that setting, don't you imagine he would consider himself fortunate for this transformation, and feel pity for the captives?

Glaukon: I agree.

Socrates: Now . . . suppose there were honors and awards among the captives, which they granted as prizes to one another for being the best at recognizing the various shadows passing by or deciphering their patterns, their order, and the relationships among them, and therefore best at predicting what shadow would be seen next. Do you believe that our liberated man would be much concerned with such honors, or that he would be jealous of those who received them? Or that he would strive to be like those who were lauded by the captives and enjoyed pride of place among them? Or would rather take Homer's view, and "rather wish, in earthly life, to be the humble serf of a landless man" (Odyssey 11.489) and suffer whatever he had to, instead of holding the views of the captives and returning to that state of being?

Glaukon: Truly, he would rather suffer a great deal than return to such a life.

Socrates: Well, here's something else to consider. If such a man would suddenly go from the sunlight to once more descend to his original circumstances, wouldn't his vision by obscured by the darkness?

Glaukon: It obviously would.

Socrates: And so, let's say he is with the captives and gets put into the position of interpreting the wall-shadows. His eyes are still adjusting to the darkness, and it may take a while before they are. Wouldn't he become a laughing-stock? Wouldn't they say, "You have returned from your adventure up there with ruined eyes!" Would they not say that the ascent was a waste of time? And if they had the opportunity, do you supposed that they might raise their hands against him and kill this person who is trying to liberate them to a higher plane?"

Glaukon: I'm afraid so.

Socrates: Then, my friend Glaukon, this image applies to everything we've been discussing. It compares the visible world to the underground cavern, and the power of the sun to the fire that burned in the cavern. You won't misunderstand me if you connect the captive's ascent to be the ascent of the soul to the intelligible world (τὸν νοητὸν τόπον). This is how I believe, and I shared it at your wish, though heaven knows whether it is at all true. Regardless, it appears to me that in the realm of what can be known, the Idea of the Good is discovered last of all, and it only perceived with great difficulty. But, when it is seen, it leads us directly to the finding that it is the universal cause of all that is right and beautiful. It is the source of visible light and the master of the same, and in the intelligible world it is the master of truth and reason. And whoever, in private or in public, would behave in a sensible way, will keep this idea in focus.

Glaukon: I agree, to the extent I can manage to understand.

Socrates: Stay with me, then, for another thought. We should not be surprised that individuals who have reached this level might be unwilling to spend their time on mundane affairs, for would it not be that their souls always feel a calling to the higher things. If our illustration holds true, that would seem quite likely.

Glaukon: Yes, likely indeed.

Socrates: Now, would it be at all surprising for one who has been engaged in the contemplation of holy things, when he ventures into ways of degenerate humanity, to appear ridiculous in his actions? What if, for example, while his eyes were still adjusting to the mundane gloom, he would be forced to appear in court to hold forth about the mere shadows of justice or the other shapes that flitted across the wall?

And to engage in debate about such concepts with the minds of others who has never beheld the Ideal Justice?

Glaukon: It would not surprise me the least.

Socrates: But one who has his wits about him would remember that there are two things that pain the eyes: being brought from darkness to light, and transitioning back from light to darkness. Now, considering that the soul experiences the same discomfort, this man would not make light of another when he met with a confused soul. He would take the time to understand if that soul was coming from a luminous realm and his eyes were blinded by darkness, or whether journeying from the darkness of ignorance into an illuminated state had overwhelmed his eyes. One, he would consider fortunate. He would pity the other—and if he laughed at either, it would be less justified if he laughed at the expense of the one who was descending from the light above.

Glaukon: That's a fitting way to put it.

Socrates: Of course, if I'm correct, then some of our educators are mistaken in their view that it is possible to implant knowledge into a person that wasn't there originally, like vision into the eyes of a blind man.

Glaukon: That's what they say.

Socrates: What our message now signifies is that the ability and means of learning is already present in the soul. As the eye could not turn from darkness to light unless the whole body moved, so it is that the mind can only turn around from the world of becoming to that of Being by a movement of the whole soul. The soul must learn, by degrees, to endure the contemplation of Being and the luminous realms. This is the Good, agreed?

Glaukon: Agreed.

Socrates: Therefore, of this matter itself, there must be a craft of some kind, which would be a most efficient and effective means of transforming the soul. It would not be an art that gives the soul vision, but a craft at labor under the assumption that the soul has its own innate vision, but does not apply it properly. There must be some kind of means for bringing this about.

Glaukon: Yes. Such a craft must exist.

Copyright © 2016 Plumbstone Books

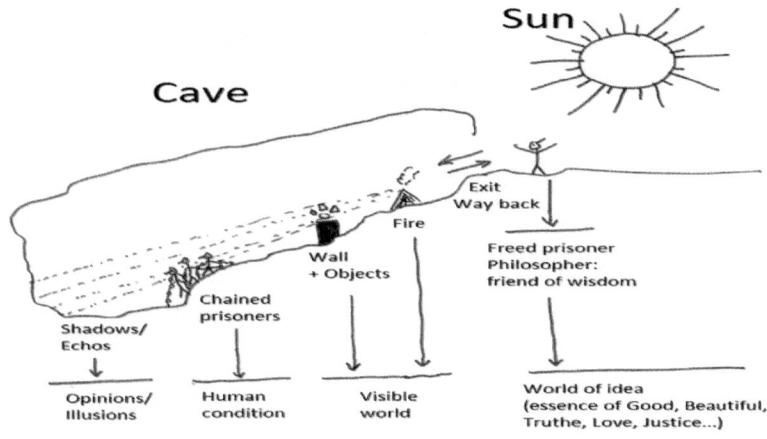

I also read Aldous Huxley's 'The perennial philosophy'

"An inspired gathering of religious writings that reveals the "divine reality" common to all faiths, collected by Aldous Huxley

"The Perennial Philosophy," Aldous Huxley writes, "may be found among the traditional lore of peoples in every region of the world, and in its fully developed forms it has a place in every one of the higher religions."

With great wit and stunning intellect--drawing on a diverse array of faiths, including Zen Buddhism, Hinduism, Taoism, Christian mysticism, and Islam--Huxley examines the spiritual beliefs of various religious traditions and explains how they are united by a common human yearning to experience the divine. The Perennial Philosophy includes selections from Meister Eckhart, Rumi, and Lao Tzu, as well as the Bhagavad Gita, Tibetan Book of the Dead, Diamond Sutra, and Upanishads, among many others.

A brilliant book worthy of anyone's bookshelf, it was because of this book that although it did not contain specific answers, it did show me paths to understanding, so I then started to read Religious texts, I read the Bible from cover to cover. I realised that there were truths in it, but a lot was written in some kind of code, you needed to be able translate it to unlock the meaning, I could not get on with it and so I didn't feel it helped me either.

Then I turned to the eastern religions/philosophies, I bought a book 'The Upanishads' a translation by Eknath Easwaran.

"In the Upanishads, illumined sages share flashes of insight, the results of their investigation into consciousness itself. In extraordinary visions, they have direct experience of a transcendent Reality which is the essence, or Self, of each created being. They teach that each of us, each Self, is eternal, deathless, one with the power that created the universe."

I was reading this as I was travelling to the Far East, to see if I could find inspiration and answers there. This is the book where the words really 'opened me up'. I felt that I completely understood 'what' they were talking about. I recognized that they were talking about 'Home' I felt and 'saw' a light shining brightly in my solar plexus area in my mind's eye. It was a powerful feeling. I knew I was on the right track and needed to follow it.

> *"An immediate practical consequence for human happiness is that the reason we try to get pleasure from outside satisfactions is we are victims of an enormous fallacy: we believe there **is** an "outside" apart from us. But we carry the world within us, and thus the source of all human fulfilment, all Love, all creativity."*
>
> *(From The" Upanishads" on The Aitareya Upanishad- by Eknath Easwaran pg 123)*

But, there was no practical way of reaching 'Home' no step by step guide, now I realized I had 'found' home, I understood I needed to get back there, but how? It was clear to me in my mind and my 'expanding' understanding that in these Eastern philosophies meditation was the key, which was the path I needed to follow. Nowhere 'outside' of me was fulfilling my need for answers; I needed to go 'inwards' not 'outwards' as implied by the quote above.

I travelled to Taiwan, my idea was to get a job teaching English, and use the money earned to go out and travel around Asia, going back to earn money again to fund further travelling. I didn't particularly like living in Taipei and met other travelers who went there to do the same as was my idea, to teach and fund further travel. There I met someone who was going to travel to Thailand, he had been there many times, living and teaching, and so I decided not to stay in Taiwan, but to travel with him to Thailand. I had the strangest but most wonderful experience as soon as I set foot on the ground in Bangkok airport. I felt like I had 'come home', I had the feeling of being at home there, and I just 'knew' that everything would be alright for me there and I felt a great 'weight' lift from my shoulders there in the airport. I never did get to teach whilst in Asia, but I did then spend a year in Thailand. Whilst there I learned about Buddhism, which I felt a connection with, and It has a very clear and easy method to follow regarding Meditation, and with the Jhana's *(The Buddha called the jhanas the cornerstone of right concentration, which is the eighth factor in the Noble Eightfold Path to freedom from suffering—and he described mastery of these states as a key to reaching enlightenment.)* of which are 8 levels, after which one goes over to another level when one then becomes an Arahant (enlightened one) I list the levels below:

Jhana with form:

1) **First Jhana:** mental activity, joy, and sense of well-being
2) **Second Jhana:** delete mental activity, leaving joy and sense of well-being.
3) **Third Jhana:** delete joy, leaving equanimity and sense of well-being.
4) **Fourth Jhana:** delete sense of well-being, leaving absorbed equanimity.

(*arupa jhana*): absorption without form, or the immaterial Jhana's:

5) **Fifth Jhana:** *jhana* of boundless space (*anantakasa*).
6) **Sixth Jhana:** *jhana* of pure expansive consciousness (*vinnana*).
7) **Seventh Jhana:** *jhana* of pure emptiness (*akinci*, lit. "nothingness")
8) **Eighth Jhana:** *jhana* beyond perception and nonperception (*nevasannanasanna*)

I list the levels of Jhana because I will refer to my experience of the levels in a short while. After I came back home to the UK, and was practicing meditation, I had another profound experience. At some point I had a 'knowing' that I needed to become a Buddhist monk, so that I could spend as much time in meditation as possible as I was having 'success' with my practice. But realized I needed many hours of practice to reach the 'goal' of enlightenment, which I saw as where I would get all my questions answered, it came as another feeling of light powerfully in my solar plexus area. It then took me 10 years to be 'ready' to actually go and ordain as a monk in a monastery. First I was recently married, to a lady I met in Thailand, we stayed together 5 years then divorced, but it was still another 5 years after that for me to have the courage and be 'ready' for 'exposure to expansion' and ordain.

Expansion of awareness of a wider reality

Meditation and monastic experiences

I ordained in the Thai tradition of Forest Monks, which is a contemplative order of Thai Buddhist monks. There is another order in Thailand of monks who care for city and country temples and service the laity with rites and rituals and study the Pali canon more than practice the contemplative side, these monks wear the orange robes you often see in Thailand and on Television regarding Buddhism in Thailand. My order wore the brown robes of the forest monks.

Whilst in the monastery I recognised perhaps the *3rd Jhana* of equanimity and feeling of well being, and just generally enjoyed the life and my continuing practice. Then about a year after being in the monastery I had a very profound meditational experience, which I believe to be the *8th Jhana*, which is beyond perception and non-perception. I will attempt to explain the experience here, but can only allude to it by allegory or simile:

*'Imagine that you are in a cave, so dark and so quiet that you have lost yourself, or any idea or semblance of yourself, in fact, it is like you do not exist at all. But, that you are on the edge of a great lake of water in this great cave. The water is so still, that you are completely unaware of its presence, as there is no sound or feeling of it at all. But then, there is a sound, it is like someone has thrown a pebble into that great lake. Now that pebble has made waves, ripples in the water. Now that there was a sound, you become aware that there **is** sound, and then slowly as the*

ripples spread out, touching other sides of the shore of the lake the other senses return. And now you are aware of yourself again, aware of the consciousness, being aware of sound. Now you are aware of consciousness being aware of all the senses of feeling. Then you become aware of the fact that until that moment of sound returning, there was no self awareness, or of thought, and therefore no senses, because they are attached to consciousness, it was as though the lake was consciousness. And in fact only in retrospect before it was disturbed there was perhaps only awareness.'

Such is the difficulty of putting spiritual experiences into words, which is why the Buddha never talked directly about enlightenment, but only encouraged everyone to practice, and to know by directly experiencing enlightenment themselves.

At this point my awareness and being is 'expanding' a lot more than previously, clearly I was then ready to receive more understanding and an expansion of awareness of a wider reality.

Empathy (relates to clairsentience)

Description - Empathy is the capacity to understand or feel what another person is experiencing from within their frame of reference, that is, the capacity to place oneself in another's position. Definitions of empathy encompass a broad range of social, cognitive, and emotional processes primarily concerned with understanding others (and others' emotions in particular). Types of empathy include cognitive empathy, emotional (or affective) empathy, somatic empathy, and spiritual empathy.

One of the 'expansions' of awareness I developed was empathy, but, it is much deeper than just, intellectually 'feeling' the suffering of others. It is being *empathic* on the level of having the emotional *feelings* and even *physical responses* to those feelings as well as thoughts, *literally*. It could be positive feelings as well, but for me, the ones I noticed were normally more of the painful type.

One example: this is the first time I realised I had developed this awareness. I was sitting in the Sala (dining and meeting hall in the monastery) and it was a Sunday. Before lunch is eaten, messages are read out, a senior Monk reads out the messages from the assembled laity, regarding birthdays, memorials of one's past away or whatever else people wanted them to say before the food is offered first to the Monks and Nuns, then the assembled laity gets their food. I was feeling kind of depressed as people were coming in and we were waiting for the event to begin. It got worse as time went on, and I felt this great feeling of loss, like some loved one of mine had passed away and I was feeling the pain of that, the empty feeling in the stomach, the wanting to cry. The notes were starting to be read and eventually the senior monk got to one, which was for a lady who's brother had just passed away in a car accident, the feelings inside were rising to a crescendo, then a lady at the front of the assembled laity burst out crying. I then realised what was going on, I was feeling what she was feeling. I felt some relief, as it wasn't my depression and feelings of loss, I realised it was this lady's, once I had realised this, all the feelings began to ebb away until I was back in a normal equanimous state. I was relieved and amazed all at the same time when I managed to digest what had just occurred.

On contemplating this new expansion of awareness and what it meant, I realised that it reminded me of an experience I had soon after I was ordained as a novice at the monastery and this experience may have been a precursor to the previously mentioned new level of expansion. One day I felt the need to see and talk with someone. I wandered around to see the normal people I would talk to, but none could be found. I started to feel rather lonely, and realised that there was a horrible feeling of loneliness coming over me, so I went back to my room and picked up a book to read to try and escape the feeling. But then when I realised that I was trying to escape this terrible lonely feeling, the words of my mentor started to ring in my ears, that this was "a golden opportunity", to understand myself. So I put the book down and just sat there, I sat with the feeling and let it take over me. Then I tried to understand it, to understand **why** I felt this way, and what caused it?

As I sat there I realised that I put a lot of store in other people, I put my safety or escape in the fact that someone was always there to talk to, when I felt lonely or needed someone to help take the feelings away. I put, as they explained in the monastery, my **center** in something 'outside' of myself. I was taught that one needs to find the center in one's self, the place of calm when all about is a storm, is a place within one's self. If when meditating or meditate walking, and I felt 'centred', it's a place in my solar plexus where I felt this feeling. I realised that *I* needed to *be* the center and that I had actually without realising it placed my center in others. So when I felt that loneliness I immediately went out to look for solace in another person, but because I couldn't find anyone I felt lost. So I needed to make myself the center for when I needed it and not outside of myself. Because everything is subject to change, and is impermanent, it's not always there when you need it if you put your center *outside* of yourself, but it is always there if the center is **within yourself**. So I sat there and realised why I had this loneliness, because I had my center outside of myself. I sat there and watched this feeling, as it didn't have the same effect on me now I knew how it came about. The interesting thing is that I saw it, and I watched this *feeling, or emotion* as it as it slowly went away. Now I saw it from a different perspective, it was like a separate entity to myself. I knew why I had felt lonely, so why was it still there? The effect was lessened but still it was there. I watched it with great interest as it slowly went away. It was like a **thing** a **separate** thing to myself, I felt it, and it was effecting me internally, but it was **not me**, That's right, it was not me. I didn't own it. So are emotions and feelings something we let in to ourselves? due to some reason, but they are not ours, they do not belong to us, but just visit us and are let in by some state of mind? In this case the loneliness was let in by the fact that I had put my center in others and not myself. This had allowed that emotion to come in, and even though once I knew what and why I felt that way, I had to wait for the emotion to go of its **own** accord. So I sat and watched it leave, astonished at the realisation of what had just happened. We believe in our emotions so much, believing that they **are** us. We even **identify** ourselves with the emotions, like **I am** Lonely, or **I am** angry, but truth is, we are **not,** we are just identifying ourselves with it, so that we **believe we are** it, we become Lonely or we become angry. Once you see and **realise** that, their power over you is reduced. What a revelation, the repercussions of this revelation were interesting. It seemed that now I was able to become calmer and not so angry, I didn't get affected so much by most things anymore, because I knew the reality and nature of emotions and was much more prepared for them. I could still get angry or sad etc of course, it is in the nature of being human, but because of my *realisation* of the nature of emotions my life and reactions to these states improved.

Telepathy (I also think is a facet of Claircognizance)

Description: direct transference of thought from one person (sender or agent) to another (receiver or percipient) without using the usual sensory channels of communication, hence a form of extrasensory perception (ESP).

I think in relation to the empathic nature of the expansion of awareness, comes telepathy, so before is the sharing of emotions and physical sensations, and thoughts, being related to feelings as both are interpreted by the mind are a natural companion in my view. There was occasion also when I would know what someone was thinking, I had some experience with this before the monastery, but again after my time there and intensive meditation it was heightened. My experience of knowing what people were thinking was also not all the time but only rarely, and I have no seeming control over it. But the way it presents itself, was not literally *hearing* the voice of someone else in my head or theirs, but was like someone had *told* me *before hand* what they were thinking, but, that I had forgotten and I was now retrieving the memory of what they said. So I didn't hear them speaking, but just my own mind repeating back, but not really in words either, it is more just a *knowing* of what was thought. In the case of the abduction or close encounter scenario with ET's, mostly people say that there was communication with the ET's but it was telepathic in nature. This would also lend support to the notion of a **Multiversal** plane of consciousness shared by all, whereby language is transcended and unnecessary. It would also explain why the contact was telepathic as in my experience; you have 'a knowing' of what is being communicated and language is not required, because it is conducted on a level where all beings are one and connected in the wider reality.

Spirit possession

I used to go for a short 40 minute nap after lunch, which was the last meal of the day for the monastic's until breakfast the next day, and it was on one of these naps that I had a most unusual experience. I had settled down on the small mattress on the floor of my room and was letting myself go. I was not asleep yet, but in the in-between state in which many experiences can come when the still conscious mind is touching on the subconscious. As I lay there on my left side a strange feeling started to come over me. I heard a voice which said "hello me old mate", but this voice, I could hear it, but not in my head, I could actually *hear* it. Then I realised that the voice came out of my own mouth. I then also noticed that my face kind of scrunched up a bit and my back started to arch, like I was an old man, it became clear that whomever this spirit may be, was taking over my body and speaking to me using my own vocal chords. This just felt creepy it was a bit too much for me and when I realised what was happening I kind of tensed up and managed to push the spirit out of my body. After a minute to compose myself and let the experience of what just happened sink in I thought "no. I can't have that, it's too much". So I said out loud "don't do that again, I don't mind if you are friendly, but don't try to take over my body, I don't like it". Whoever the spirit was certainly seemed friendly and said hello in a way as if he *knew* me. But I did not recognise the voice or feel any recognition of who this spirit might have *been.* The spirit never tried to take over my body again. He may have been around, but that was the last direct contact I felt from this being. But those 40 minute naps turned out to be very eventful times.

Ghosts

Whilst on one the subject of spirits I should mention Ghosts, this is just one experience of a handful of such experiences I have had with the phenomenon. I was on a trip with my Thai girlfriend, we were invited to stay overnight at a friend of hers house along the border not far from an official border crossing with Malaysia at Hat Yai in southern Thailand. We were with a few other people and as the Thai's are actually quite conservative, the men would sleep in one room and the ladies would sleep in another separate room.

 I went to shower and clean up before bed. In Thailand you find houses that have a kind of big water container, which is not a bath, but with a bowl you scoop up the water with and then proceed to pour it over yourself to bathe. It's always hot especially right down in the south of Thailand so cold water is a blessing before bed to cool your body down. So as I started to pour water over my head I heard a 'ching' sound. At the other end of this water container, which is made of concrete and has a 4 inch thick wall, on top of the wall about waist height is the bar of soap in a metal dish. Now this container is about 6ft long and I was standing at one end of it and the soap dish was at the other end. It sounded like I, or the water had knocked the dish and made the sound. But I didn't splash myself that hard, and it seemed like it was too far away to have been splashed. I stopped and thought for a moment then thought that I must have splashed the soap dish. I tried to put it out of my mind and went into the room I was to share with another man, I was alone and decided to try and rest and 'Meditate sleep'. This means to lie down meditating and to just let yourself fall into sleep. Then as I was laying there I heard something, it was a voice, but it wasn't outside of myself it was in my mind, I listened and heard a female Thai voice speaking to me. My Thai was not good enough to understand what she was saying, but I got the *'impression'* that she was asking who I was and what I was doing there. It was just a kind of *'Knowing'* of what she was saying as if we connected on some level beyond the language barrier (there was an element of telepathy here). I came back to the very conscious level of being awake and sat up on the very thin mat on the floor which was the 'Bed' for the night. I then looked around and said out loud in my best Thai "My name is Trevor, I'm from England, here as a friend of my girlfriend, and I'm staying for one night and then going on tomorrow." I knew this was out of the way of tourists and perhaps a white foreigner had never stayed in this house before. The spirit must have been confused and intrigued as to who I was and what I was doing there. I remembered a time in my past when I lived with my Thai wife in a village in south east Thailand outside of Chantaburi. There were very few foreigners that ever went there at that time in the early 1990's, I stayed in the village for some months and attracted a lot of interest because of being so white and foreign. There was a lady in the village that was quite scared of me and use to call me "The white ghost" as she believed I must be a spirit of some kind. The amount of interest was high even in the early 1990's. So how must have this Thai spirit have felt, coming as she most likely did from a distant past?

I had hoped that she understood what I said and settled down to sleep for the night. I slept well and awoke in the morning to a bright and warm day. If I wasn't sure about what had happened the previous night, I soon would be sure as when I was sitting down at a high chair at the breakfast bar, a dark shadow went past me, visible out of the corner of my eye, at the same time I suddenly felt a cold chill come over my bare leg and hand. The spirit of the Thai lady was not imaginary or a visionary aspect of meditation, she was real, in the sense of affecting me physically. I guessed she must either be saying goodbye, or just letting me know of her presence. So she was there, but not visible, to me at any rate, is she then living in another level of multiverse, but one very close to our own, present but not fully, and able to interact in some part on this level of the multiverse?

Shamanic visions

Again when I was lying down after lunch in a very relaxed way I experienced something new. My mind was clear and everything was dark, as I lay with my eyes closed. Then all of a sudden I found myself travelling down a dark tunnel, in my mind's eye. This seemed like a narrow dark tunnel and I was shooting down it at quite a pace. I came out of the other end, into a large dark area, all was blackness, except for in front of me was a shape, not symmetrical but like a hole in broken glass in a kind of fallen over figure of eight shape or perhaps like the infinity shape. Around the edges of this shape were what looked like cracks, splitting out into the darkness. But *inside* the shape was another place entirely, it was like looking through a window to somewhere else. There was a scene, like looking at a television. In the scene was a plain of grass. And bent down on their haunches were a load of kids, dressed in scout's or Cub's uniforms. They were all searching the grass for something it seemed, but for what I had no idea. And I could see the back of an adult, standing over the kids watching them, perhaps directing them? I got the feeling this person was female, although I only saw her back, in a light brown shirt and the back of her neckerchief could be seen. There was no sound to this scene but it was in colour.

This was very intriguing, and I was fully conscious of myself and the scene. It was like one of my life dreams, with a certain *real* quality about it, it was completely lucid. I thought ok this is interesting, let's see if I can go through that window like portal area and investigate the scene from the inside. But as soon as I tried to push my consciousness through the window I was expelled from the vision and zoomed back to my room.

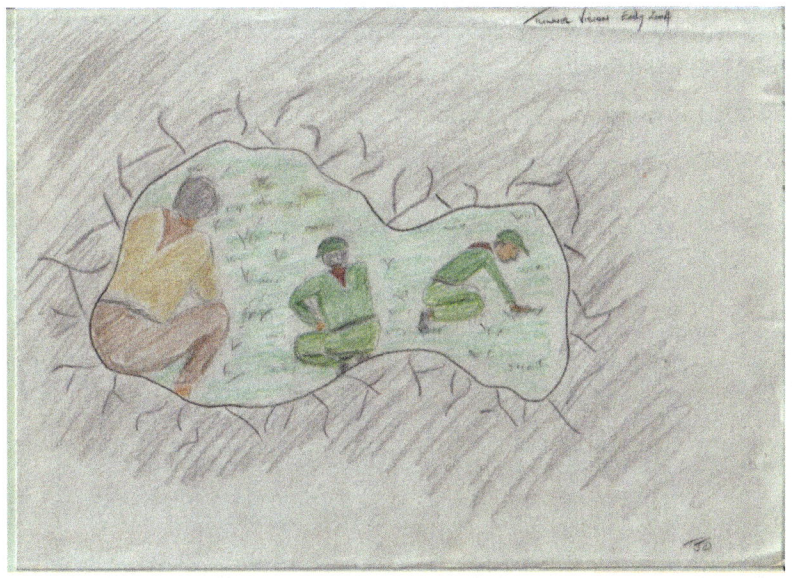

It turns out this was not a one off event, as on another day I found myself shooting down that same tunnel and out into the large inky black void. This time there was no window, but instead was an amazing sight. Hanging in the inky blackness was no less than Stonehenge! But the massive stones were not just floating around in space on their own, they were all still firmly on the green grass of ground we know them to be on. But the ground only extended just outside of the stones, then the ground underneath was dark earth that tapered down to a point directly underneath the middle of the circle approximately slightly deeper than the stones were tall on the surface. But there was one very obvious difference to the stones, on one of them was what looked like etched into the face of the stone was a spiral? All of this vision was simply hanging there in this massive black space. It was like I was standing at the edge of a massive cavern containing all this as when I looked down I could see those cracks again. Like the darkness had been hit and had the splintered cracks like seen on a glass window that has been hit hard and hasn't broken, but cracked all over. These cracks went off into the distance towards the hanging Stonehenge, but disappearing from view before getting that far. What could this mean? There must be a purpose, a reason for seeing this? I decided to try and walk on the cracked blackness with my mind, but as I did I again was expelled from the area and back into my room.

Although these two events seemed like they must be important, or showing me something of value, I couldn't work it out. I discovered that American shaman Indians use to have the same experience of shooting down the narrow tunnel and seeing the future through a window, or getting some answer to some question. I had definitely never heard of or read of this before, and found that particularly interesting that I should have a shared experience with shamans of Native American Indians. This puts their experience into an interesting new light as they were obviously telling the truth. But why should I experience that? Was I a shaman in a past life? Or a common experience to mystics, shamans and spiritual practitioners the world over? These places one visits, could they be other existing universes within multiverse?

Shamanism and the Multiverse

(By *Ariel Barriero http://www.thepittpulse.org/shamanism-and-the-multiverse*)

Are there traversable universes outside of our local universe? The story of the "Ant of Knowledge" tells the tale of how ayahuasca, an Amazonian vine with hallucinogenic properties, came to be. A vegetalista shaman — a shaman who gains their powers through plants — rode on the back of the ant as it told him the ayahuasca vine was born of the "dust and pollen which cling to a sticky substance coming out of the ant's body" and that thousands of years ago, the ants were intelligent beings. Asteroid collisions destroyed their cities, and the ants became smaller and smaller, losing their imagination while becoming robotic and the species we recognize today.

Shamanism is considered to be the most ancient religion on Earth. While there are plenty of Western (new-age) adaptations these days, they mostly lend to the bastardization of early religions, and strip from them the truly spiritual connection and experience. Furthermore, Western cultures discredit shamanism as baseless science, but this attitude is founded in the demonization of cultures that were brutally colonized by Euro-American invaders.

Shamans are considered renaissance people in their villages — healers, doctors, psychiatrists, therapists, musicians, actors... the list goes on. One of the principal ways the shaman gains these abilities and their breadth of knowledge is through their "spirit" helpers — and we must use the word spirit loosely here, as it does not mean the same to them as it does to us. Spirit is essence, and it is in everything. In order to gain a spirit guide, shamans must visit another world. "The Siberian shaman's soul is said to be able to leave the body and travel to other parts of the cosmos, particularly to an upper world in the sky and a lower world underground."

..............There are many interpretations of multiverse theory, but publications by physicist Max Tegmark generated a strong distaste for it in the astrophysics community. The Feynman path integral, however, can offer a more reputable argument for this case. The Feynman path integral "accurately predicts the behavior of any quantum system... but it is more of a philosophy than a rigorous recipe. It suggests that our reality is a sort of blending — a sum — of all imaginable possibilities." This observation supports string theory, where any decision anyone has ever made leads to two worlds being created, resulting in an infinite number of universes simultaneously existing.

.... What the shaman does, perhaps, is leave the physical behind and use a wormhole to travel with their soul. If a shaman's soul leaves their body, might it be the size of a particle? Dr. Perdomo called this the spirit voyage, or astral projection as we know it in the West. Sacred geometry is used in Indian cultures as well, where shamans see mandalas in their travels.

There are several accounts of the many worlds through the shamanistic religions, and there are many physicists trying to prove the existence of wormholes, parallel universes, and multiverse theory. The shamanistic religions do not need our scientific proof to make these theories valid; these studies and mathematical proofs are for our own peace of mind in Westernized society. Are we shutting down our greatest form of study by referring to shamanism as primitive and false? "An emphasis of what can be seen and measured may, though, shut out what religious adepts such as shamans claim to 'see' as they break through to different states of consciousness."

Surfacing memory of my 1977 UFO sighting

As all of these experiences unfolded, with my deepening practice and the expansion of my experiences within the wider reality, my understanding and connection to this wider reality was increasing. With this came a memory recall of my 1977 encounter with the UFO. It was whilst asleep that the memory returned. I saw the UFO in the sky that day, but before that event, at the same time further back down the road, I had seen the craft landed in a field. I remember going towards a metal gate and on the other side was the craft, although I could not see the craft in my recall, I 'knew' it was there. I climbed over the gate and coming towards me was this beautiful lady, in a all-in-one blue, tight fitting suit, she had blonde hair in a bob style down to her shoulders, she was coming towards me with her arms outstretched as if she was going to pick me up. She was smiling broadly and as she got closer I noticed one of her hands, and it had 6 fingers on it. I don't remember being picked up, I just remember the emotions I felt. It was a very strong feeling of love, connection and belonging. These words really do not impart the intense feelings that they really were, I had never felt this love and connection and belonging before, it was like those words and associated emotional feelings were all wrapped up in one feeling, one emotion. So deep and wonderful, I had never experienced feelings like that before, and in the rest of my life till now at 59 years of age, I still have never felt anything like it, and I know I won't until I meet with these beings again. I believe these beings reside in a higher frequency range than the normal range of frequencies we on earth live in. As she approached I was hit with this higher frequency level of beautiful emotions that she emanated, I don't think you had be empathic to feel it, either, you just had to be in their presence within their field of resonance. These higher frequencies I believe are part of the multiverse in which these and other beings live in. I believe she was with two males, I didn't see them, but again I just *Knew* they were there, it was part of my memory, but not visual so perhaps held back for some reason. So I concluded that the memory of the bird of prey that landed on my shoulder was indeed the *'metaphor'* cover memory of this physical meeting with the occupants of the UFO. The craft came down, we met and 'said hello' I don't recall the full memory of that encounter, but I 'know' I went on board, and of course they then 'flew away'.

Another encounter

Whilst I was a novice at the monastery, I got to take my Mentor and Teacher to a house that was left to the monastery by a benefactor for a private 10 day retreat. My mentor was to have a silent retreat and I would make him breakfast and lunch and attend to his needs. I would knock on the door to give him his breakfast and Midday meal and he would take it, all without speaking. This house was only about 1 mile from Rendlesham forest, where coincidentally the UK's most famous and well recorded apparent UFO encounter took place. A UFO was seen on 2 nights in 1980 in the forest outside RAF Woodbridge which was operated as a "twin base" (twin airfield) with RAF Bentwaters, and as a single unit with Bentwaters under the 81st Tactical Fighter Wing. Woodbridge Air force base was occupied by the 67th Aerospace Rescue and Recovery Squadron, which answered only to the Department of Defence in Washington D.C. also unknown to the people of the UK at the time, was the fact they was holding nuclear weapons, and quite possibly the reason for the interest shown by the possible ET's/ UFO. This was one of the best recorded cases in the UK and even the world due to the number of reliable and trained observers of military personnel that witnessed and chased the UFO through the forest. An audio tape was also recorded by Colonel Charles Halt as he led the team through the forest which is undeniable proof of the incident, alongside the paper trail left as they reported the incident to Washington and the UK MOD. It is worth noting that this area of Norfolk is a 'hotspot' for UFO activity and in fact all sorts of paranormal activity. As legends of for example 'shuck' a large black dog which rampaged through the local towns, is a historical record, and other strange creatures seen in Rendlesham forest.

   The house was on its own, not far from the sea, in fact when we arrived at the house we sat up drinking tea and looking out at the sea from the upstairs studio window. The benefactor was an artist and had a studio upstairs. It also had a bedroom upstairs next to the studio where Ajahn Nyanarato (my mentor) was to stay. I had a bedroom on the ground floor. That first night we stayed up until midnight, chatting and drinking tea, Ajahn was to start his 10 day silent retreat the next day. I was meditate sleeping and was not yet asleep when I saw through my closed eyelids a light flashing around. As I was in a semi-conscious state I ignored it. But then there was flashing again that I could see through my eyelids. So now I was in a much more aroused state. Then by the time the lights were seen for a third time through my eyelids I was totally awake and conscious. This time I wondered what was going on and opened my eyes. To my surprise the room was full of light. This light was not a normal torch or headlight kind of light, but extremely bright, brighter than daylight, and a very white light. It completely filled the room. My bed lie along the back wall and at the foot of my bed was the doorway. On the opposite wall to the bed was a window. Through this window is where the light appeared to be coming in, as I could see that the curtains were lit up from behind. There was no sound and I could hear no one moving about. Then all of a sudden, it was as though I blinked, and the light was gone. I was sitting up in bed and now a bit afraid to move. I studied the doorway to my room waiting to see some movement or hear something, to be honest I was waiting nervously to see a short alien figure walk into the room, but there was nothing. I felt rather afraid, but eventually I lay back down and managed to fall sleep.

   Outside the window to my room about 5 feet from the window were large fir trees; the next day I checked out the area and found no footprints or car tracks. I figured it couldn't have been a car coming down the track shining its headlights into the window because these large fir trees were in the way. The light could only have come into the window in the way it did from directly above the house. If it were a helicopter I would have heard it, there were helicopters that flew in from the sea and towards the old military base on occasion which were Chinooks and you could hear them from miles away, so I would have heard one of those if it was hovering over the roof of the house. No, whatever it was was totally silent.

There was another thing now as well; I could feel a presence in the house, just in the downstairs of the house. It was a strong presence, so strong that I could point to the exact area in a room where this invisible being was. Not only that, but I felt that it was short, at about 3 to 4 feet tall, it was all extremely bizarre and unsettling. I felt that the white light was connected to a UFO, but at the time in my mind, I only thought that the presence I felt in the house was of a ghost or spirit. For some reason I couldn't connect the two events together? I didn't realise the effect the presence had on me until the night time, as I found that I was afraid to go to sleep, and was also afraid of being on my own in the dark! So much so, that I had to leave a light on at night for the remainder of the 10 days I was to stay at the house. "But I'm a grown man", I thought to myself, it's ridiculous, never the less, I had to have the light on and felt afraid. Something had definitely happened that night. At one point I decided to sleep upstairs on the sofa that was in the studio outside of Ajahn's room, because of the feeling of the presence downstairs and the fear of the night I felt. I couldn't talk to Ajahn, because he was on his retreat, and what would I say? It would sound ridiculous! I would have to wait until he finished his retreat and ask him if he saw anything that first night. So I felt better upstairs, safer, and tried to settle down on the sofa. But I couldn't, I just felt uncomfortable, *something* was stopping me from being able to sleep? It became so bad, it was giving me a headache, and making me so uncomfortable that I knew I would have to go back to the downstairs bedroom. I also felt that this was what the being downstairs *wanted.* That somehow it couldn't watch me if I slept upstairs and so it wanted me to sleep downstairs. Although I really didn't want to, I eventually gingerly went back downstairs to sleep in the bedroom on the ground floor, the effect it was having on my mind was stronger than I could resist. This is how it was for the next few nights, and during the day I could feel a presence at certain times. Once Ajahn had finished his retreat I asked him if he remembered seeing any strange lights on that first night, or any sounds. But unfortunately he said he didn't hear or see anything. I explained what happened and about the feeling of a presence that I felt downstairs. Ajahn said he would meditate downstairs and see if he could *feel* anything there, but although he said he may have seen a light, apart from that he said he felt nothing. But actually the feeling of a presence was gone some days before. On the last day before we left the house Ajahn said we would do a chanting for the spirit if there is one there, I agreed and felt better for doing it. So we chanted a few parittas (prayers) before leaving. I was to investigate my feelings and meditate on the incident with the white light, and found that I *felt* like it was someone who for some reason had detected my presence there and had come down to investigate. Then upon realising it was me, felt satisfied in a way of 'oh, it's ok it's only Trevor' and then left. It seems strange but this was the feeling I was left with. Not a scary feeling of having been abducted, but is what the evidence points to. I think that because of the presence of the 'invisible' ET I was taken somewhere, which is why it was necessary for me to be 'watched' for 3 days, but I still have no recollection of the event of being taken to this day.

The presence which I thought was a ghost or spirit on reflection looks also typical of an abduction scenario, as sometimes people who have been abducted have said that one of the ET's is sent to 'observe' the abductee for three days after the event. I also think the ET was getting my conscious mind to believe it was a ghost whilst it was there, as it was powerful enough to render itself visually invisible to my mind, as well as strong enough to make me sleep downstairs even though I didn't want to. The purpose is unknown, but believed by some, and I agree with this, to be as a protocol to make sure the subject has not been harmed by the procedure and has settled back into their environment comfortably. Even perhaps to make sure the incident is not reported and made a subject of investigation, which it wasn't of course because of the situation. And the presence was only there for three days; also the presence was giving the strong impression of a being of small stature, which again lends support to the ET theory as many reports of short ET's abound, especially in the abduction field.

My mentor Ajahn Nyanarato told the Abbott of our monastery 'Luang Por Sumedo', who is a very experienced Monk and also believed by many including myself, through my interactions with him, that he is actually 'enlightened' about my experience. Luang Por meditated on it, and it was reported back to me by Ajahn Nyanarato, that a 'very powerful' being had indeed visited me that night in the house we were staying in. That was a nice confirmation for me, as Ajahn himself did not experience anything himself. I felt that the ET did not want to disturb Ajahn's retreat, and maybe its presence upstairs would have disturbed him, which is why I had to sleep downstairs.

Vibration and Frequency

One time I was lying in my bed at the monastery trying to sleep at night, but I just couldn't sleep all night, maybe sporadically I did manage some sleep, but it didn't 'feel' like it. I just could not pinpoint however 'what' was stopping me from sleeping? Then all of a sudden in the morning *it* stopped, the *'it'* was vibration. The whole of my body was vibrating, it felt like every molecule of me was vibrating, the only reason I knew it was vibrating was because it all of sudden *stopped* vibrating. What was the cause or reason of the vibration? I personally believe it was because of my spiritual endeavours, was I literally raising my vibrational level? I also think that there is a strong possibility that other 'beings' may be involved in this 'raising of vibration' especially with my history of ET contact and the other previous possible abduction event. Maybe I am receiving help along my journey by friends who reside in different levels of the multiverse?

Encouragement

Something else happened that made me wonder about receiving help from beyond the physical plane. One day I was waking from sleep in my room at the monastery and I could hear a voice, not like the voice of the spirit that was trying to possess my body as before. This time it was in my mind, but not my imagination, I could tell, the experience is totally different and it was a female voice. This voice was singing, it was a simple song, something of what I could remember before it faded was something like "you have to be strong, to be good, you have to be good, to be strong ..." I don't recall more of the song, but I think that it repeated, then the voice faded out as I was becoming more conscious. So this voice, this being, was singing to me in my sleep. The voice was like nothing I had ever heard in my life. It was the *sweetest* voice I had ever heard. It was such a beautiful experience it brought a tear to my eye. I believe she was singing a song of encouragement, to help me to carry on with my chosen spiritual path. But who was that being singing? Maybe I have an idea now of whom it might have been, which will be revealed later on, but at the time it was just an amazing experience. Experiences such as this are also known as 'clairaudience'.

Clairaudience definition

The power or faculty of hearing something not present to the ear but regarded as having objective reality.

'Taken from www.merriam-webster.com/dictionary/clairaudience'

Hearing angels sing spiritual meaning
May 4, 2023 by SM

Have you ever heard the singing of angels? Although it may seem like a far-fetched idea, many people think that angels exist and can interact with us through music. Hearing angels sing is frequently regarded as a spiritual experience that can have a profound effect on our lives. This article will look at the **spiritual significance of hearing angels sing** and how people who do so might find inspiration and direction.

Hearing Angels Sing Spiritual Meaning

The expression "hearing angels sing" is frequently used to indicate a powerful spiritual encounter. It stands for an experience of intense spiritual connection or being in the presence of something bigger than oneself. A sense of joy, serenity, and love are frequently felt along with the experience. It is said to be a sign from the cosmos or a higher power letting someone know they are on the correct track or that they have a unique task to do. Although the experience may vary from person to person, it is frequently referred to as transformative and life changing.

Understanding the concept of angels: Angels are said to be spiritual creatures who serve as guides and messengers for a higher authority. They are considered to provide consolation and direction to individuals in need and are frequently connected with love, light, and protection. The general notion is that angels are kind entities who may assist us in overcoming the difficulties of life, however other religions and spiritual practices may have their own interpretations of what angels are.

Hearing angels sing: What does it mean?

Many people report hearing angelic music or singing during moments of spiritual awakening or introspection. This can manifest as a feeling of euphoria or peace, or even a physical sensation such as chills or goosebumps. Some interpret this experience as a message from the angels, or a sign that they are on the right path in life. Others simply see it as a beautiful and meaningful moment that brings them closer to the divine.

'Taken from https://spirituallymeaning.com/hearing-angels-sing-spiritual-meaning'

Discovering who I really am and our place in the multiverse

Early 2018

I had a bad cold or flu, and not sleeping very well, this was in early or late January. And whilst I was in an in-between state, but conscious, in a state rather like in a meditation, a vision opened up in front of my mind's eye. It was a swirling tunnel with gold and black colours, the tunnel sides were mainly gold, with black interwoven between the gold, swirling around like the tunnel was made of liquid with the gold and black moving about in it, A bit like when you see fuel or oil swirling around on the surface of water. As I was looking at the tunnel, I noticed a line of small links which looked rather like 'bubbles' going off in a straight line down the tunnel disappearing into its depths, I was surprised at this and wondered what they could be? On consideration I thought that perhaps it is the link between me and my body, a bit like the silver cord that mystics speak of in the context of dying or near-death experiences. The silver cord is also mentioned in the Bible.

'Remember your Creator before the silver cord is loosed, or the golden bowl is broken, or the pitcher shattered at the fountain, or

the wheel broken at the well. Then the dust will return to the earth as it was, and the spirit will return to God who gave it.'
Ecclesiastes 12:6-7

    I watched this scene taking it all in for probably only a moment or two. Then I heard a voice say "Do you want to go?" I paused for a moment, recognising the voice as sounding like my own? And then I replied "yeah". Then all of a sudden I took off down this tunnel at some speed, I felt like I was literally being pulled through this vortex like tunnel, body and all, as I felt the forces on my body as I whooshed around from left to right as the tunnel twisted and turned. Eventually I came to the end of my ride, and I was in what I perceived as the inside of an aeroplane or craft of some sort as it was very wide, like 20 to 30 feet wide, so much bigger than a normal aeroplane. There were seats and people milling about, all sorts of people, old, young, men, women and different cultures. I remember there was a black man sitting down in front of me, leaning forward with his elbows resting on his knees, looking like he had been waiting for ages. I was standing, apparently, looking around. They all seemed to be human looking, like myself. And then I heard the voice again, It said "Do you want to see what you look like?" I paused for a moment, thinking what a strange question it was, but decided it sounded rather intriguing and said "yes". Then, as I was looking ahead of myself, the space directly in front of me started to fold in on itself, a bit like water gushing down a plug hole but without the circling around. It was like space itself that was folding in on itself. Then out of this folding of space came a face, Humanoid, but, it was silver? I couldn't believe it, I wasn't expecting anything, no preconceptions, but I really didn't seem to be expecting a SILVER being. It had a translucent, shimmering quality to it though, very strange! I feel that he was male, he had a strong masculine face, he also had long wavy blonde hair, I couldn't see the hair, but it was a *knowing* of the fact that he had this hair. I was a bit shocked at this sight, so I started to try and get a better look, at first I couldn't see a nose at all, and it was just flat in the space between his eyes. So my gaze followed down his face and then I saw what was actually 'the end' of his nose. It was a very flat looking long nose which was squared off at the end, quite bizarre I thought. At this point I felt a bit worried, with the silver colour, and the straight square ended nose I wondered if he was an android of some sort? I found this disturbing, because would that mean I was not a sentient being? Then I looked a bit further down and I saw a mouth. It was in a small round shape, but the jaw was going up and down. Now I realised that he was talking to me, but I could not hear a word, frustratingly, this did however make me feel better, as He didn't seem robotic anymore with a moving jaw and mouth. Not that an android could not have these things, but perhaps although I could not hear what he was saying, he was assuring me that he was not an android, and I was getting the message through a more telepathic means. It was at this point our meeting came to a sudden end, and I found myself whooshing back through this portal type wormhole back to my body, still sitting up in bed.

This is the best rendition of the Portal that I can make, see the 'line of bubbles' heading off down the tunnel.

The silver being that is 'me', a representation of my primary incarnation as I perceived him, in my meeting after travelling through the wormhole.

Guy Steven Needler

I was very confused after this experience, it brought up some deep questions on the nature of my existence, such as, how am I here as myself, but also existing somewhere else as a completely different person/being, having a life somewhere else at the same time? It was very perplexing, to say the least. I found, as happens with me sometimes, that I am led to videos on the internet, or they come past me, often, until I notice them. This is how it was with a video of a man called 'Guy Steven Needler'. There was a video of his that kept popping up on my feed, I thought that it just didn't look particularly interesting, but something said to me, oh it keeps coming up, and I should give it a watch. So I did, and then it struck me, that Guy had a vast knowledge of the structure of the universe, the multiverse even, and could then possibly have an informed opinion on my experience. So in May of 2018 some 4 months later after struggling to understand what my experience meant, I found Guy's email address and wrote to him. After writing the portal experience explained above I then wrote:

"So when thinking about this I am a bit confused in trying to find an answer for myself, and this is what I wanted your opinion on, if you would be so kind. I recognise and have for some time, that these bodies we inhabit are just vessels for us, and that we are here to experience and gain 'enlightenment', 'realisation', 'truth' or whatever label you want to put on it, as well as being beacons of light and higher vibration for the rest of the planet. But why would I have and live in this vessel here on earth, but also have a different vessel somewhere else? as for me this other being, that I am, looked like it had some form, although to be fair, the silvery look could be that it is less dense and obviously of a higher vibration. But still just another form, why have two forms? I posture that as the other silver form I may not be getting the kind of experience that can be gained from having this more dense three dimensional form, and so trying or have been given the opportunity to live in this form, in order to gain an even higher vibration and ascend to the goal of what it is that we are trying to achieve? Or am I, as this other being, lying in stasis connected to some technology or awareness and living this life as a sort of programme?"

Reply from Guy: Dear Trevor,
Due to my workload I don't usually get chance to answer so quickly, if at all, But I was drawn to your text and knew exactly what was happening with you, you are a secondary incarnation. To answer you in a more complete way I have extracted the text in my book **The Anne Dialogues** to describe the detail behind the process of becoming a secondary incarnation, I hope this helps. FYI The TES is the True Energetic Self our Higher Self or Over Soul or God Head. All these names mean the same thing - it describes that much bigger part of us that remains in the energetic that our Aspect (soul) is projected from.

*"**Secondary Incarnations** Secondary incarnations are a function of the ability of the Aspect to move to a lower frequency incarnate vehicle when it incarnates into an incarnate vehicle at a frequency higher than, but including, the eighth frequency, associated with the physical universe and therefore the multiverse as a primary incarnation. When an Aspect incarnates into an incarnate vehicle that is in the eighth frequency and above, it retains most of its connectivity and functionality associated with being in the energetic environment of its TES. This*

means that the Aspect can freely commune with its TES and can manipulate its self and its environment at will. Although the Aspect is incarnate, it will be, from the perspective of those Aspects who incarnate into the frequencies that are below the eighth frequency, in the energetic state. This perception of the next level above a frequency being energetic, from the perspective of the observer is a consistent perception that starts at the third frequency level and continues upward to the eleventh frequency. Please note here that at the Earth level the first three frequencies are needed to create the environment the Earth and those components of the physical universe that are represented at this level can exist within, so there is no similar function from the first in observance of the second, to second in observance of the third frequency levels that are observed at the third in observance to the fourth and the fourth to the fifth, etc. I will reiterate again that the functionality associated with being able to create a secondary incarnation, an incarnation within an incarnation, is ONLY available from the eighth frequency and above. Getting back to the description of the functionality of the secondary incarnation then, an Aspect will actively move its sentience and associated energies from its primary incarnation into another lower frequency incarnate vehicle if it wishes to experience an existence at the desired lower level and that that experience will enhance those experiences within the primary incarnation that it would not have experienced otherwise. The experience in a lower frequency incarnate vehicle is expressed as a "secondary incarnation" and not a "subincarnation" as this is a different function, one that I will explain in the next subject heading. The Aspect that chooses to enter into the role of being in a secondary incarnation also has the ability to pass on its experiences to those other incarnates that are working with it at the frequency of domicile of the primary incarnate vehicle. This enhances the efficiency of experience by extending it to its counterpart incarnate Aspects or colleagues. When an Aspect enters into the secondary incarnation it can either leave the primary incarnate vehicle in a form of stasis, leaving only 5 percent of its sentience and associated energies in the primary incarnate vehicle in a sort of "caretaker" role, allowing it to collect the experiences of the secondary incarnation and disseminate it to its counterparts or colleagues on an automatic basis. This has the effect of the Aspect only truly experiencing one incarnation, the secondary incarnation, until the demise of the incarnate vehicle that is *being used for the secondary incarnation is experienced, wherein the primary incarnate vehicle is reanimated by the sentient energies used in the secondary incarnation returning to it. Alternatively, the primary incarnate vehicle can be left in a functional state by the Aspect leaving circa 20 to 30 percent of its sentience and associated energies within the primary incarnate vehicle and projecting the remaining energies into the secondary incarnate vehicle it has chosen. This is, although being classified as a secondary incarnation, the true state of the incarnation within the incarnation. It is classified as such because the sentience associated with the energies that animate the primary incarnation and the secondary incarnation can and does actively, effectively, and regularly migrate between the two incarnations, experiencing both and controlling both simultaneously. In this instance, the sentience associated with the secondary incarnation tends to migrate back to the primary incarnation during the times when the secondary incarnate vehicle needs to rest and remove the toxins accrued during its normal daytime animation—when it needs to sleep. An interesting but basic fact of the use of the secondary incarnate vehicle is that it is regularly monitored by the Aspect's counterparts or colleagues and is accessed for information on the levels of integration and functionality expected/experienced by the Aspect in animating it. To do this the vehicle used as the secondary incarnation is removed from its environment (when necessary), it is monitored and information downloaded from it that is useful to the primary incarnation and/or its counterparts/colleagues. This action is one that is experienced on a regular basis and is the explanation for the experiences of many, but not all, UFO abductions reported.*

Blessings and Best Regards Guy

Wow, my mind was blown!! Amazingly, Guy's words from a book he had written some years before were a reflection of my own thinking, even using the same words such as 'stasis' and for the primary incarnation to have experiences in the lower frequency life that can't be had in the primary higher frequency existence. Also that the secondary incarnation is monitored by colleagues to make sure the functionality and experience is going according to plan, hence why sometimes I could have been taken, which has also been my experience with UFOs. I realise now that I knew some of the answers guy has provided here, because *'I am' the* person that I met, so obviously we are an intertwined being sharing the same consciousness.

Mary Rodwell

Later, on the 23rd august 2018, I was lucky enough to have a regression session with Mary Rodwell, she has done hundreds of regression sessions with people over the years, many can be found online. She has written several books on the ET subject and has talked at many conferences. I really like her approach to the subject and especially as she is one of only a few well known researchers in the field connecting all the psychic, spiritual, paranormal and other fringe subjects into the same arena, realising and finding links that they are all connected, the more holistic approach to all these subjects that many others try to separate. Groups of people insisting that fairies, earth spirits, dragons, mediumship and life after death are separate and nothing to do with ET's, abductions etc are just narrow-minded and refuse to accept that people with NDE's (near death experiences) for example can often see small grey aliens in their tunnels of light etc. But they are all residing in the multiverse, in planes of existence just outside of our own. I started a conversation with Mary in 2017, regarding information she had, and sharing some of my own experiences. I said I would love to have a regression with her. Then in 2018 the chance arose as she was coming to the UK. Strangely I didn't want to regress to the meeting I had with my 'other 'self, but instead my first 'remembered' close encounter with a UFO and its occupants when I was 12yrs old, back in 1977. But in the course of the regression, Mary asked about two UFO's I saw, as we had chatted before the regression, to find out what I wanted to get out of it and where I wanted to go with it, so I had mentioned these sightings to her. The first sighting was in the daytime on the day I left the Buddhist monastery where I was ordained as a Buddhist monk. I spent 3 years at the monastery which was in Hertfordshire UK, and the second sighting was at about 4.30am in the morning when I was on the way to work as a delivery driver in Kent UK, which was obviously dark at that time. The UFO was very visible both times, stationary in the sky, it was constantly changing shape, and changing colour, if I remember rightly it was a kind of Orange, green, white and maybe blue. Interestingly, both times I was driving when seeing them, so no chance of taking a photo, not that the idea of taking a photo entered my head, I was just amazed to see them. I saw the first one as a 'nod' to me that I was going in the right direction in life, as in leaving the Monastery and back into society. The second one, I think it was just to confirm they are always there watching over me, that I am not alone, and probably was another reason from the first time I saw them as well. So Mary asked me, to ask where they were from, as in that regressed state, you can ask questions to get answers, from the craft, the occupants or whoever you are interacting with, or even your higher self. I asked and had an answer come to me, and I replied 'Aldebaran', I was confused as I didn't really know much about it, but I had heard the name before. Mary said, "Yes, it's a star". So that was very interesting, I did wonder if I was also from Aldebaran, hence why they were showing themselves to me and letting me know they are watching over me? I found more information on Aldebaran but I don't think my primary incarnation is from a planet near there, but may have lived there at some point. There is more information I found that I will mention a bit later on.

My drawing of the Crafts seen leaving the monastery, and later in Kent, a poor reconstruction though.

Guy Steven Needler and the structure of the Multiverse

At this point I believe that I need to set out the structure of the multiverse, as understood by Guy, which has helped me to understand my position and indeed all of humanities position within the Multiverse. This is very important knowledge for us to understand and contemplate in my opinion. I will be using slides that guy has used in his lectures, and drawing heavily on his work, I will put links to Guys books and websites etc at the end of this book so the reader can further their knowledge and understanding.

A little about Guy taken from his website

Guy Needler MBA, MSc, CEng, MIET, MCMA initially trained as a mechanical engineer and quickly progressed to become a chartered electrical and electronics engineer. However, throughout this earthly training, he was always aware of the greater reality around him as he caught glimpses of the worlds of spirit. From his teens to his early twenties, these glimpses drew him to read extensively the spiritual texts of the day, and meditate intensively. Then, he was told by his guides to focus on his earthly contribution, so he subconsciously scaled back the intensity of his spiritual work. When Guy reached his late thirties, he felt the call to return to his spiritual roles. The next six years saw him becoming a Reiki Master and pursuing a four-year commitment to learn energy and vibrational therapy techniques from experts in the fields. He studied with Helen Stott, a direct student and teacher of the Barbara Brennan School of Healing™ (BBSH) methodologies. As a prerequisite for attending BBSH based courses, students were required to pursue personal development and psychotherapy via various methodologies like the Pathwork™ methodology described by Susan Thesenga and other methodologies developed by Donovan Thesenga and John and Eva Pierrakos. His training and experience in energy-based therapies has resulted in his being a member of the Complementary Medical Association (MCMA).

During his training as an energy healer (1999-2005) Guy discovered that he was able, via meditation, to traverse the frequencies above those associated with the Auric layers. It was during these "trips" to the higher frequencies that he discovered he could communicate with the energetic entities that existed on the various levels of our multiverse. These entities included the OM, beings created from the energies of the original manifestation who pervade the omniverse that is the Origin, the creator of the God of our multiverse, the Source Entity, its peers, the co-creators, and the creator of the co-creators itself, the Origin (referred to as the "Absolute" in Hindu texts).

So from here I will continue with his understanding of the multiverse and our place in it, which answers a lot of questions of my experiences, and also hopefully maybe that of some of you, the readers too.

(A 'beyond the source production'.copyright © Guy Steven Needler. All rights reserved)

What is a multiverse?

Multiverse vs. Universe

- **Multiverse**
  - Belongs to **Our Source Entity**
  - Structured
  - Made up of ***all* the Universes** in our Source Entity's *control*
- **Universe**
  - Equals **One Frequency Level** (Also referred to as a Frequency Band, or Environment) **containing a number of Sub Frequencies**

    e.g. A Frequency is like a Radio Bandwidth which contains a number of Radio Frequencies within the Bandwidth

History of God Workshops and Traversing the Frequencies are a 'Beyond the Source' Production. Copyright© Guy Steven Needler 2012, All Rights Reserved

The source, (our source entity which is number 1 of 12 of such source entities) of which is known to humans on this planet, as 'God' in religions. The source has created the multiverse within itself, and our universe is of the lowest frequency levels of all the universes in the multiverse.

> **Frequency Bands**
>
> **Frequency Level** or **Frequency Band** is a:
> - Form of Energy
> - Environment
> - Condition for Energies to exist within
>
> The **Multiverse** combines **Frequency Levels** to make up **Dimensions**

This is different to what we have been told and educated regarding the makeup of reality, and *our* universe regarding dimensions, it will be explained as we go along.

(A 'beyond the source production'.copyright © Guy Steven Needler. All rights reserved)

The Multiverse and Dimensions

- **12 Dimensions** exist in **Our Source Entity's Multiverse**
- Each **Dimension**, *except our own – the First* has the following structure
  - Made up of **3 Sub-Dimensional** components (Described as 'Tritaves' in channelled communications)
  - Each **Sub Dimensional** component is made up of **12 Frequency Levels**
  - **One Dimension = 36 Frequency Levels**

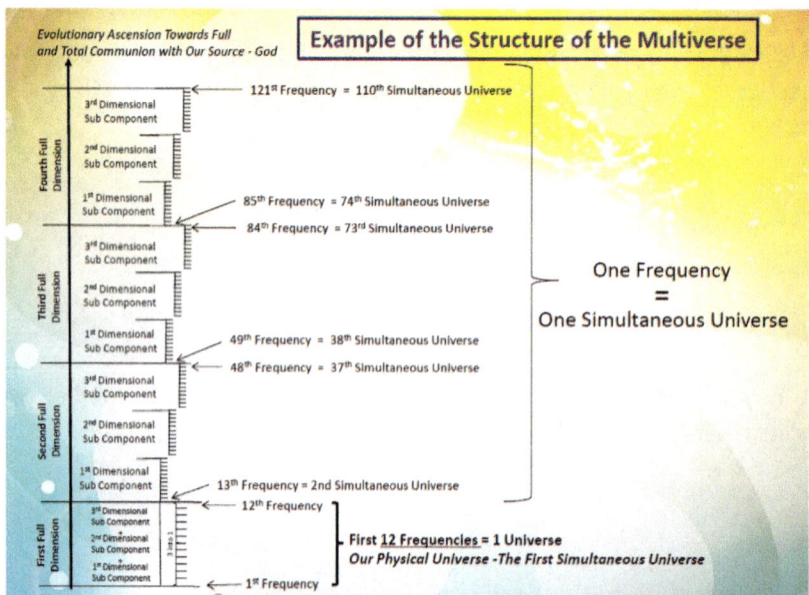

So as you can see from the diagrams, one dimension is made up of 3 sub components, and each sub component has 12 frequency levels, remembering that 1 frequency level is a whole universe in its own right. So 1 dimension effectively has 36 universes, each universe above the previous one is also much 'larger' than the previous Frequency level or universe. In fact everything, as you may have noticed is in powers of 12. The increasing infinitude of each universe or frequency level is the same, so each universe is 12 times bigger than the previous one below it. Just have a quick think about the size of *our* universe; you can't really picture it, can you! Also it is correct to say that scientists only measure our universe in what they call *'the known universe'* because, they do not know the actual size of it, with each expansion in technology they can see 'further' into our universe. But so far the 'edges' of it elude us.

These frequency levels or universes are also completely self-contained, simultaneous, manifest universes in their own right. The upper frequency levels or universes are *not parallel universes,* that is another thing entirely where 'event spaces' are created through our choices which create localised, suburban sized, city, country, planet, galaxy, universe or even multiverse sized event spaces. But the explanation of that is beyond what is needed for the explanation of our place in the multiverse, and I recommend going to guy's information for more on that subject.

Our Universe in the multiverse

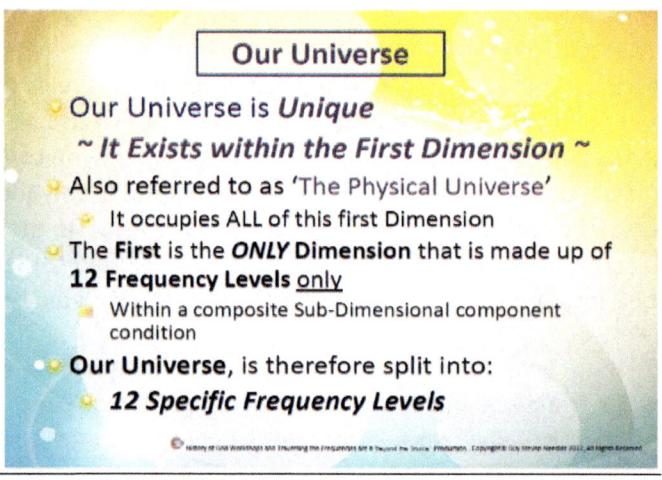

So our universe is different to the all the other subsequent universes, because it is made up of the lowest frequencies. So the 3 sub components have collapsed into 1 composite sub dimensional component, allowing only 12 frequencies to be created, and the 12 frequencies are so low, that they are *all* required in order to create one universal environment. The subsequent frequency levels (universes) have so much more infinitude that they can house the basics required to create a universe, so that the 13th frequency in the first sub component of the second full dimension is a complete universe in its own right, and so on for the rest of the frequencies to the top of the 12th dimension.

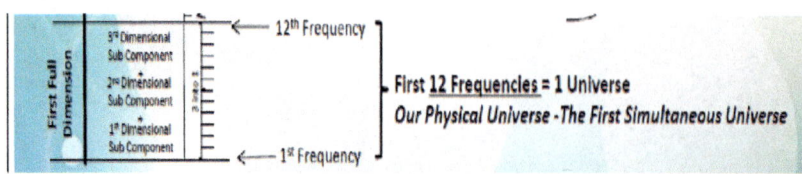

(A 'beyond the source production'.copyright © Guy Steven Needler. All rights reserved)

What are Aliens?

Further to understanding the structure of the Multiverse, it is important to discuss and understand what aliens/ETs are and what their role is in relation to us. Here again I am using Guy's information and slides to explain.

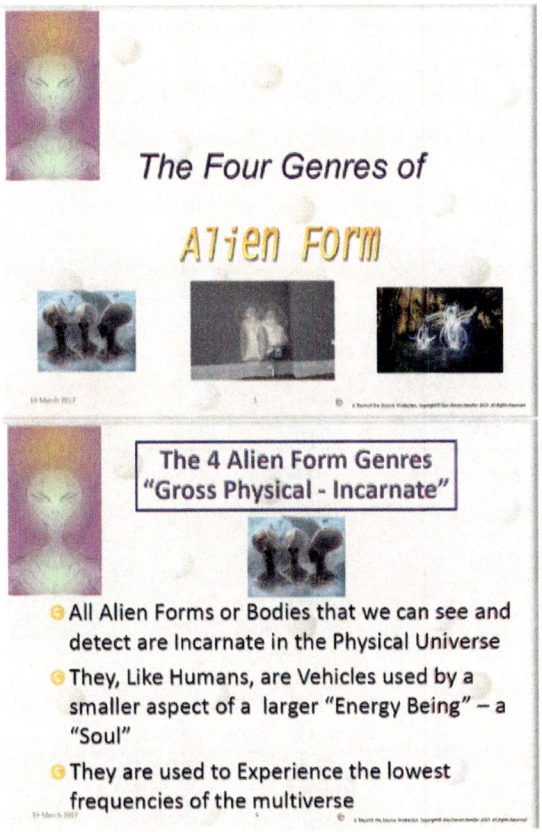

So we humans like the aliens are smaller aspects of a much larger being, which itself is a smaller aspect of an even larger being, which is the source or what religions call God. So we are aspects of what Guy calls the TES (true energetic self) or what is also known as our 'higher self' or the Hindu's call the 'Godhead' or Dolores cannon called the 'over soul' it is the bigger part of us that remains disincarnate and retains about 70% of what we are.

Why are we incarnating into this low frequency universe and not the higher different parts of the multiverse? Well, it's because we are helping our higher selves to evolve, and as aspects of our higher selves we come to this lowest part of the multiverse because we can experience, learn and evolve in an accelerated way through hardship and difficulties, part of which is because this is of such a low frequency plane of existence we are almost 'cut off' from our higher selves. It is rather like operating on a 12k modem compared to a Billion k or more connection when in the higher frequency realms, so we are operating on much lower 'bandwidth' of understanding and knowledge. What we see is limited by our own gross physical eyes, in a narrow band of the spectrum of light.

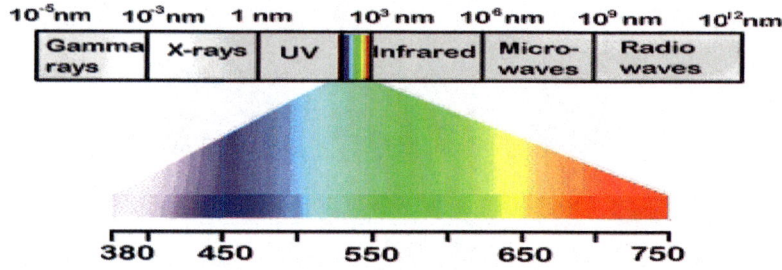

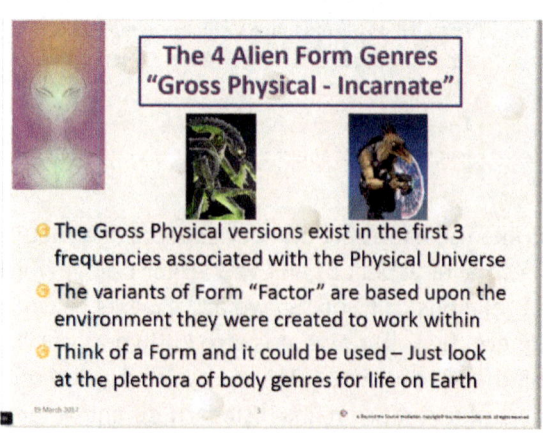

(A 'beyond the source production'.copyright © Guy Steven Needler. All

rights reserved)

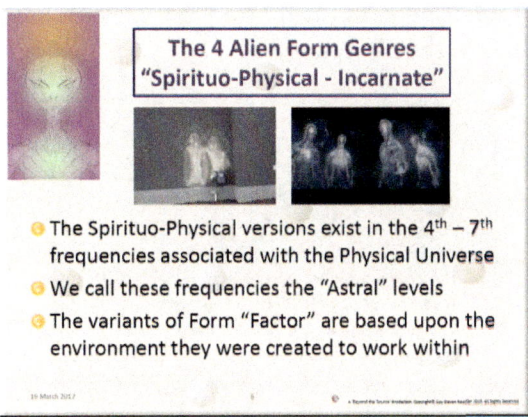

What is beyond that narrow band of our vision is undetectable, it's still there, but we don't see it. Humans tend to think that what we don't see, we tend not to believe in. Unless some technology comes along that detects it, such as radio waves all the way along to Gamma rays and so then we can see it's there. We know we have a gross physical body because we can see and feel it.

The first of the incarnate vehicle alien bodies is in the physical, the human form is created with 10 energy or frequency levels. The first 3 are the gross physical, the next 4 are the physico-spiritual or sometimes called 'the astral', and the next 8 to 10 are the spiritual levels. All of those 10 frequencies allow some form of incarnation. Above these levels are in the energetic, and are outside the need to incarnate into a physical body.

In the spirituo-physical levels, it should be noted that often people clarify the 4th as the lower astral, sometimes it is classified as the Astral itself. In Guys understanding the 4th is the lower astral, 5th is the upper lower astral, 6th is the lower upper astral and the 7th is the upper astral.

So the aspects of the higher self that have incarnated into a vehicle in the 4th frequency to experience physical incarnation are in a frequency *above* us in the 3rd frequency and so are invisible to us. Those incarnated aspects in the 4th frequency can however see us, they are walking around us right now, and they are here all the time. Those who incarnated in the 5th frequency can see those in the 4th and 3rd frequency. But the aspects in the 4th frequency like us in the 3rd cannot see those aspects in the 5th frequency.

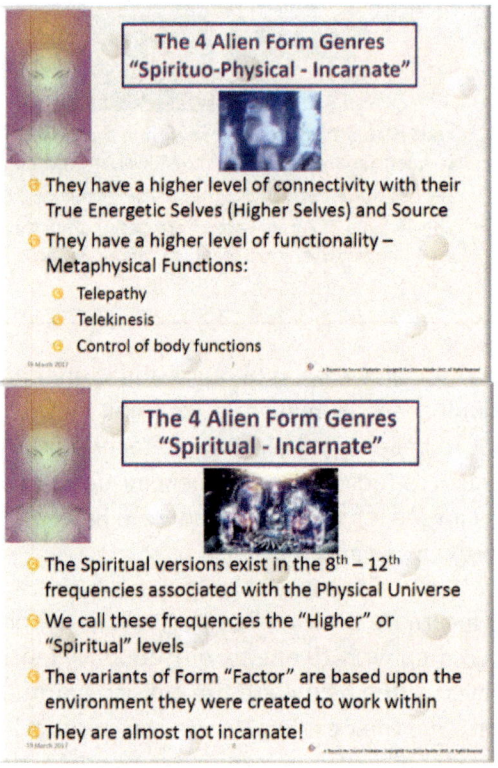

From the 4th frequency up to the 7th frequency, those incarnates start to have control of their bodies, they start not needing gross physical energies and nutrients such as eating and drinking. They start to use energies directly from energy centres called the chakras. There is a marked difference from the 4th compared with the 7th frequencies, if they decided to let us be aware of them they would start to seem like gods, they could manipulate things and move things with a force, but they are still an incarnation. The beings that have incarnated in to the 8th to the 10th frequency levels are in the higher spiritual realms. When you go from the 6th and 7th levels into the 8th to 10th frequency levels, it is almost as if it is not incarnation, it is as though the body almost does not exist. Those of us that are able to link into these incarnate beings on these levels will be able to be aware of their presence, but will not be able to 'see' them. So aliens in the 8th to 10th levels are almost not classified as incarnate, but they will still be there.

If you think about the thousands of different form factors of life here on earth from humans to fish to insects and birds etc there is an extremely wide variety of forms. That is just an indication of the myriad of different types of forms that exist throughout the universe. So if you think about the different levels of gravity and living environments found throughout the universe you get form factors that are designed to be able to live in those different environments, and so there are many variations on what we call the human form.

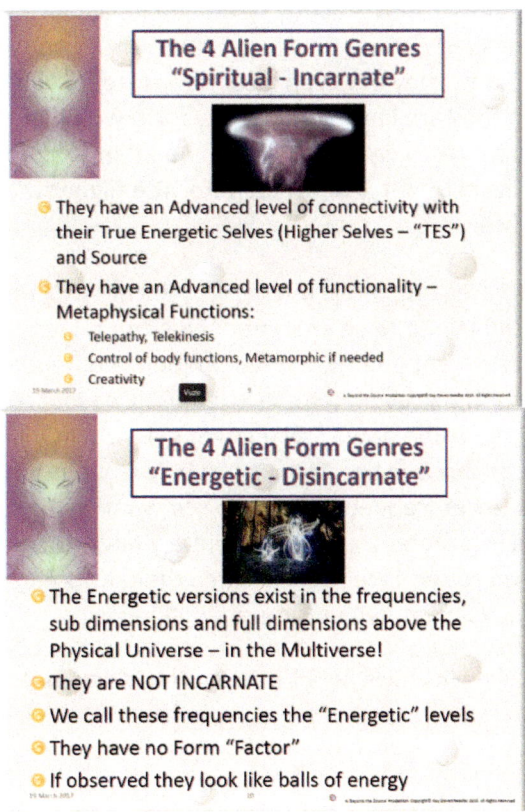

The incarnates in the 10th to 12th frequencies the 'spiritual' types are almost totally connected with the rest of themselves to their 'true energetic self', that big part of themselves that is always disincarnate, always in the energetic and always in the Multiversal environment. They know who they are, what they are and what they have to do in their incarnation and are able to navigate their way through their incarnation in a Karma free way. By not getting addicted to the thoughts, behaviours and actions associated with being in a low frequency environment. They maintain themselves in a way that is consistent with their environment.

Metaphysical functions they are working with means that telepathy, telekinesis and creativity even are secondary. Communication with other versions of themselves, body types and individuals across different galaxies are not a problem for them. They know who and what they are, they know they are in an incarnate state for a certain period of time and when they are leaving. The body form would be amorphous, its body would be much lighter, and they would only be tactile within the frequency level that it is incarnate into. The higher the frequency the finer they are.

The fourth type are completely energetic, they are aspects of sentient energy projected by our 'true energetic selves' or higher self into a smaller unit of sentient energy just to experience different parts of the multiverse, sometimes even here. We definitely cannot see these, but sometimes if they come down low enough in frequency we can see them as an amorphous mass. And we can before we incarnate come down to these lower frequency levels to see what we are going to get into before we incarnate here. They definitely have no form factor but if they come down to this level we can catch them on some cameras and they look like balls of energy or 'orbs' if you like.

(A 'beyond the source production'.copyright © Guy Steven Needler. All rights reserved)

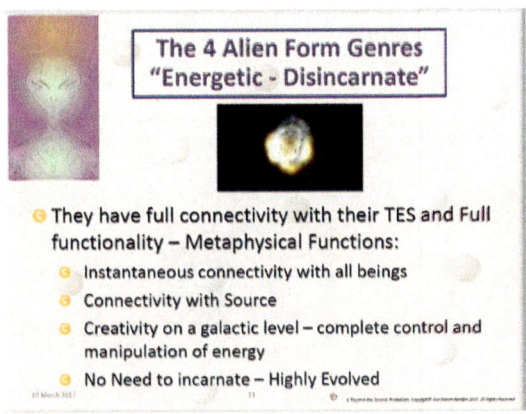

These beings are totally connected and everything they can do in the energetic is done by pure intention and pure thought. Instantaneous connectivity with the TES or higher self and source (God) and instantaneous connectivity with the universe. They can do anything they need to, they can create planets or star systems if they wanted to and they are very highly evolved.

So basically what we have are 4 body types

1) Gross physical – the first 3 frequencies associated with the physical universe
2) Spirituo-physical – the next 4 frequencies (4th to 7th)
3) Spiritual – From the 8th to 12th frequencies
4) Purely energetic – which go above the 12th frequency and therefore go the next full dimension

Three Genres of Alien vehicle (UFO)

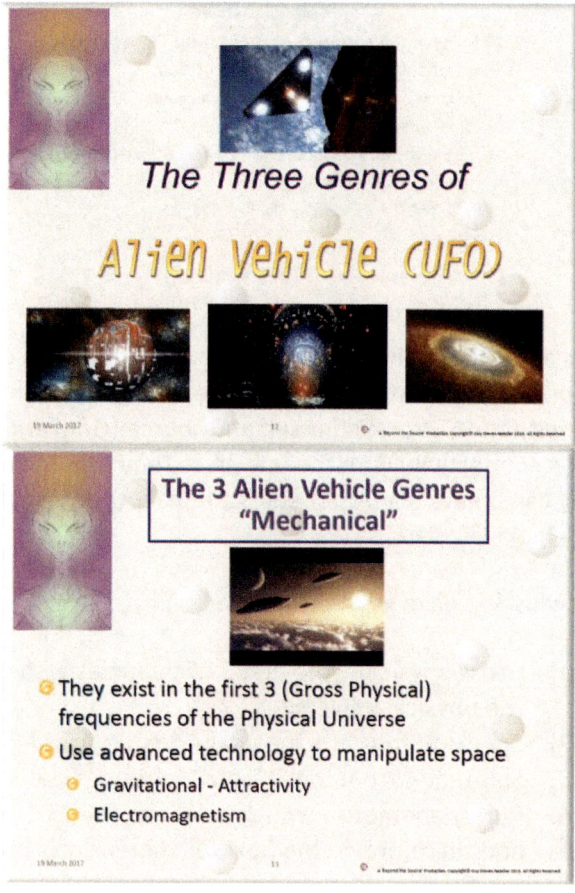

Lets look at the main genres of vehicles used to move around:

When you are in the gross physical we see UFO's with all sorts of shapes such a saucer, triangles and cigar shapes. They move around by using mechanical means, in essence they use technology to move around.

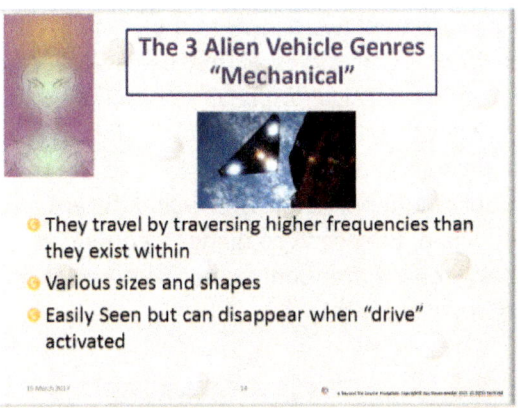

(A 'beyond the source production'.copyright © Guy Steven Needler. All rights reserved)

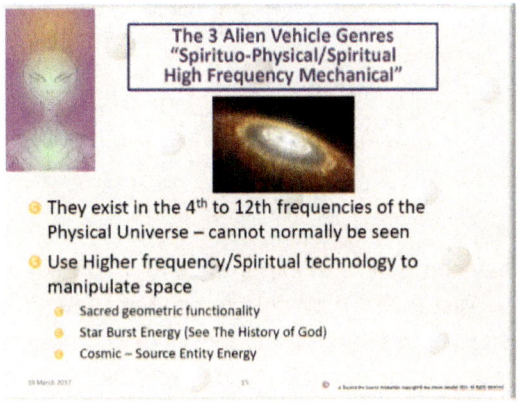

They can use Gravitational – attractivity or by electromagnetism and they can move around very quickly from one frequency to another. They tend to shortcut the point from A to B by increasing their frequency to enter into a higher frequency and finding an exit point in that frequency to re-enter our frequency which makes them appear to move in seconds or 'instantaneously'. They can travel from one side of our galaxy to the other side in seconds or a couple of days depending on their technology, but basically they can move extremely quickly. When they go to move and activate their drive, they just seem to 'disappear' as they enter a higher frequency.

The next vehicle type is with those beings that live in the 4th to 12th

frequencies which are the Physico-spiritual body types, and also including the 'spiritual' body types as they use a similar sort of vehicle. It can be a mixture of mechanical or pseudo energetic / biological energetic if you want to call it that. They can't normally be seen in the gross physical universe, the only time we can see them, is when they come down to our frequency level. They use different frequency levels to move around again, they can use higher frequencies or they can even find the gaps between the frequencies or 'frequencies between the frequencies' to move around.

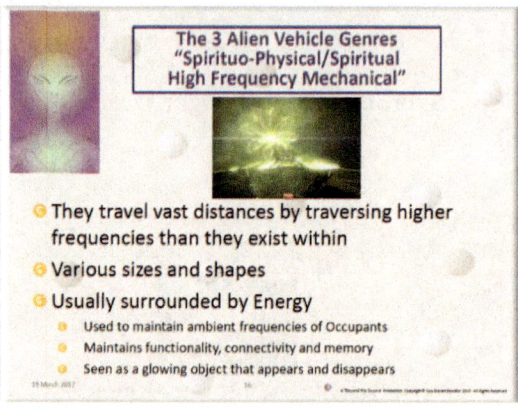

Interestingly they come here to experience learn and evolve as well, but they do it from a distance. To be able to do that they have to enter our environment, so they use varying technologies such as sacred geometry, or moving the ether using cloud bursting technology which allows them to be in our frequency, but maintain their own high frequency level. So when we come down here into a physical body to experience, learn and evolve, we forget who we are, and we become almost totally absorbed into our incarnate state, believing our human bodies is 'who we are' and a temporary personality called 'the ego' is created. And as we grow in age we become immersed in 'who we are' and we don't connect with, unless we are trained to do so, with our higher selves, or with other individuals who are incarnated or those who are disincarnate, so we haven't got that capability. So if we incarnate into a body in a higher frequency and came here to this frequency, we would need to protect ourselves and would need to protect the higher functionalities of communication and functionality. So those vehicles that are mechanical or pseudo-biological or pseudo – energetic tend to have some sort of shielding to maintain their frequency level.

We actually do this ourselves, for example an aeroplane maintains a lower frequency environment in the cabin so it can move around in a higher frequency or rarefied atmosphere to move around and come down again. Also, a submarine maintains a higher frequency environment (air) to enable us to move around in a lower frequency environment (water). So we also use this idea of maintaining an environment that's conducive to our frequencial functionality based on where we originated from in a higher perspective to move around in an environment. So therefore it's not unreasonable to see how these higher frequency vehicles pop in and out of existence. When they come into our environment they are surrounded by some kind of light or energy field that we cannot understand or discern, or sometimes they look exactly as they, but only for a moment as they only want to experience something quickly and then they pop back into a higher frequency. If they moved out of their vehicles without any sort of protection of their frequency they would start to forget who and what they are and start to lose their functionality. They would to become a human being.

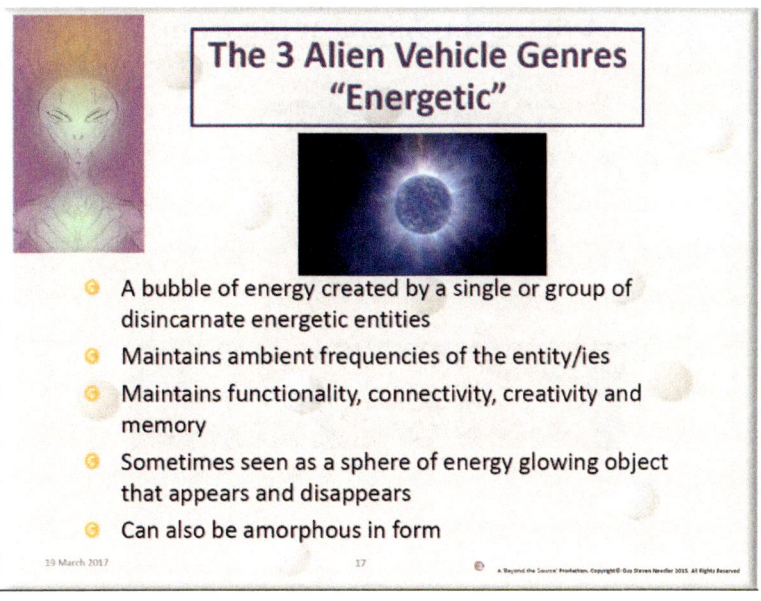

Purely energetic beings – are disincarnate, so whenever they come here, they just create whatever they need to create around themselves, a group of them may create a collective energy around themselves to move from one point to another or to move into this environment, so you might start to see larger spheres or amorphous movements of energy. Or sometimes smaller ones, sometimes we might think they are ghosts or sometimes we might think they are something else. But in essence those which are disincarnate that come here, we can't see unless they protect themselves and they start to use something that interferes with this frequency. So in essence they are creating something that is an energetic environment that protects their higher frequency.

We are seeing more of these types of things as the human race are gradually moving up in frequency and it's not just in photos, but also with the physical eye.

Where the Aliens come from

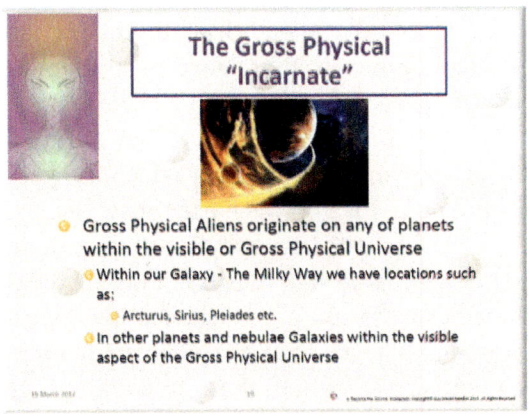

The general understanding from our perspective about UFO's is that they are mechanical, they come from the first 3 frequencies that are available to the multiverse and the first 3 frequencies of our universe, they are gross physical. They move around sometimes with higher technology but they are basically within the visible range that we see with our telescopes. Sometimes we call them Arcturians, Sirians or

pleiadians etc etc; sometimes those incarnate civilisations are in a slightly higher frequency of the 4th or 5th frequencies. In general those who are interacting with or abducted by, are those within our universal environment. They can be from the stars close to us or from other galaxies as well.

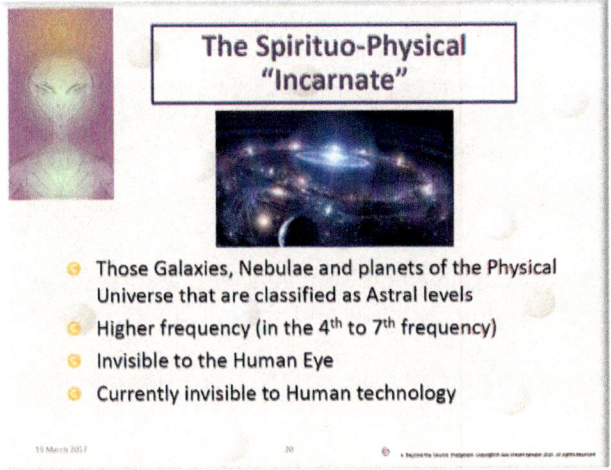

The spirituo-physical incarnate Alien is from a similar location, just that it's in a higher frequency level so that would be other planets, Galaxies or nebulae. They are there but in the 4th to 7th frequency levels of the physical universe, so we don't see them, but they are still there, in increasing levels of frequency and therefore decreasing levels of physicality. They are here now, on the earth, observing us, seeing what we are doing with our free will, because a lot of these individuals in the gross physical don't have 'free will' they don't have individualised free will. They have various different forms of collective will, sometimes these individuals are tied into a collective will, or sometimes in extreme cases it's a hive mentality will where they are working together towards a common goal. But in general these are areas of the physical universe that we don't see because they are in the higher frequencies. There will become a time when we will see them as we develop a thought process that takes us beyond the gross physicality, and we will have machines that can see them. Or people who have become self aware and self awake will see them as an overlay on the physical with their own eyes.

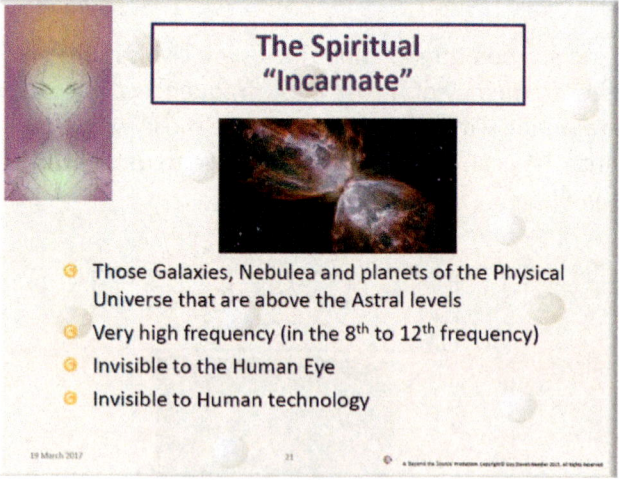

Spiritual incarnates again come from galaxies, nebulae, planets and are of the 8th to 12th frequency levels and are still in the physical universe.

(A 'beyond the source production'.copyright © Guy Steven Needler. All rights reserved)

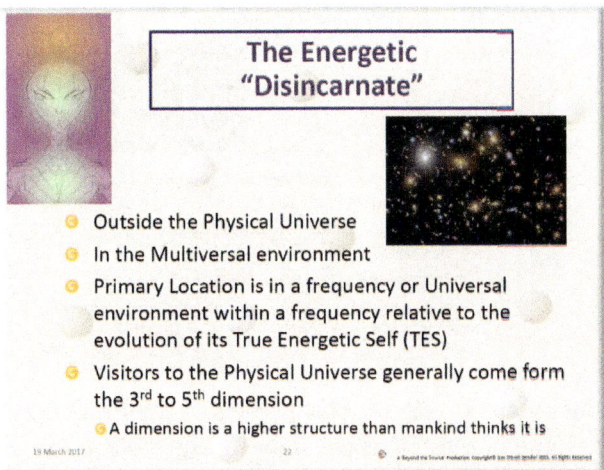

The purely energetic visitors here don't exist in the physical, they exist in ANY of those universes represented by any of those frequencies that are in the 'sub dimensions' of the full dimensions anywhere in the multiverse generally. Although it has to be said that they do, in general, as a generalisation tend to oversee individuals if they are from the 3rd to 5th dimension.

A reason for abductions

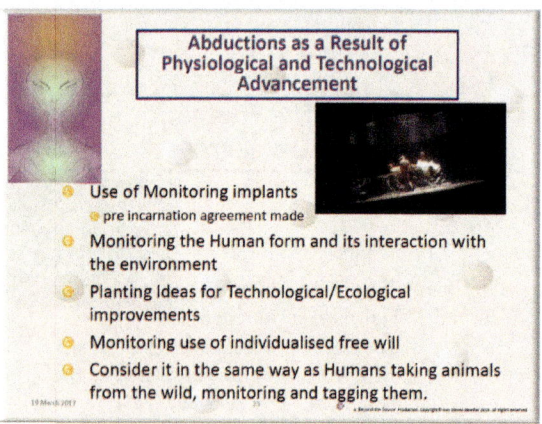

Before we incarnate we go through a series of things we want to experience, some of the things we want to experience is to be helpful to other souls or aspects that have incarnated, so that they can understand what it's like to be in this level and experience individualised free will. So we create these pre-incarnation agreements to be guinea pig, as an expression, to allow certain implants into certain monitoring systems to see how our sentient energy, our souls, are interacting with our bodies in the environments we are in, in the way it interacts with others within the environment.

(A 'beyond the source production'.copyright © Guy Steven Needler. All rights reserved

Some of these implants are monitoring how we are coping, what we are doing and how also we are dealing with the environment, like destroying or creating the environment and how we use our individualized free will So to look at it from a different perspective, scientists like to look at how animals work in the wild so they take them from the wild and scare the living daylights out of them. We poke, we prod them we take their temperature, we take their blood samples, we put GPS tracking devices on them and we send them away again. And it's possibly a different location from where we took them from so they wake up and think how did I get to this place? So if we do this to animals, it seems reasonable that we have agreed to have this done to ourselves if we are interacting for the greater good with other incarnate civilisations. We are always working together, even though we don't think we do, with other incarnate civilisations, so they are benefitting from us being here, in a very unique environment, where we are in control of ourselves individually, and in control of our environment individually.

So we have to think about aliens as another 'form factor' that we can incarnate into, they are another way we can move into this environment, so we can experience, learn and evolve in a different way. A different way to incarnate with different environments, different skills, different abilities, different levels of stress, joy, difficulties etc.

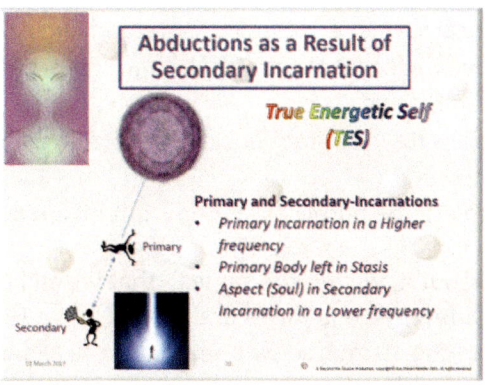

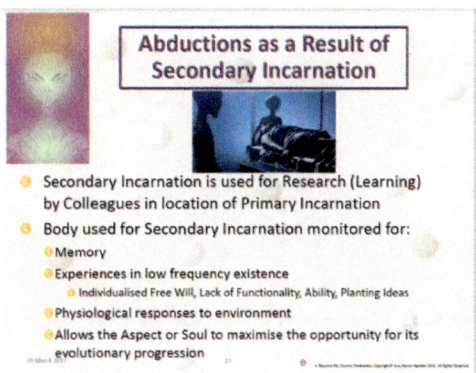

So now we get to my experience as being a secondary incarnation, as is mentioned in the slides above.

In general though a secondary incarnation is used for research, is useful for learning for those individuals who can't incarnate into the lower frequencies. Apparently to incarnate here is a bit of an honour and there is apparently a waiting list to incarnate here. As there are countless billions of aspects living in the higher frequencies/universes in the multiverse who want to experience, learn and evolve in the lower frequency environment. So this is a way that many higher frequency beings can get the needed experience through someone else's work, tapping into us either mechanically, telepathically or energetically.

- So aliens are incarnate entities (just as we are)
- Aliens incarnate to experience, learn and evolve (just like us)
- They have the same aspect (souls) and true energetic self (higher self) as us
- They incarnate in all frequencies and locations of the physical universe
- They can also be purely energetic – not incarnate

So if you think about it, we are the same in that we all incarnate in vehicles in the different frequencies and come from a TES (higher self) and connected to the source, so who really are the aliens? **We are the same, we are also aliens.**

(A 'beyond the source production'.copyright © Guy Steven Needler. All rights reserved

What are we (Humans) and how we incarnate

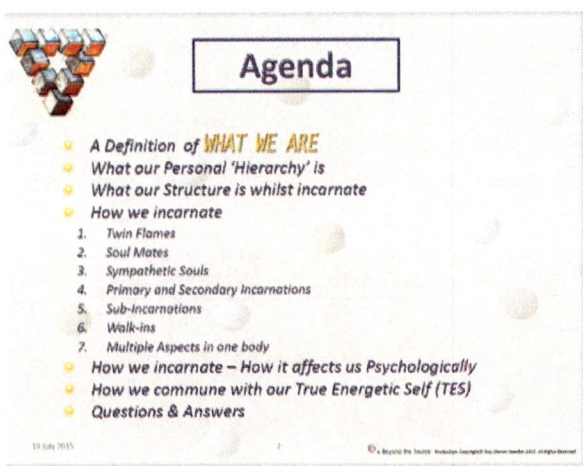

Let's go through 'what we are' and what our personal hierarchy is, because in some small way that also represents the hierarchy between the source (our creator) and what our 'true energetic selves' are. What our structure is, whilst we incarnate and how we incarnate. This is just a 'flavour of how we incarnate, it is not a full list of ways in which we *can* incarnate, there is much more to it, these are just some of the things that you will recognise. Then we will go through how it affects us psychologically when we incarnate in some of these different ways, and how we interact with others. And then how we commune with our 'true energetic self' once we finish our incarnation.

(A 'beyond the source production'.copyright © Guy Steven Needler. All rights reserved)

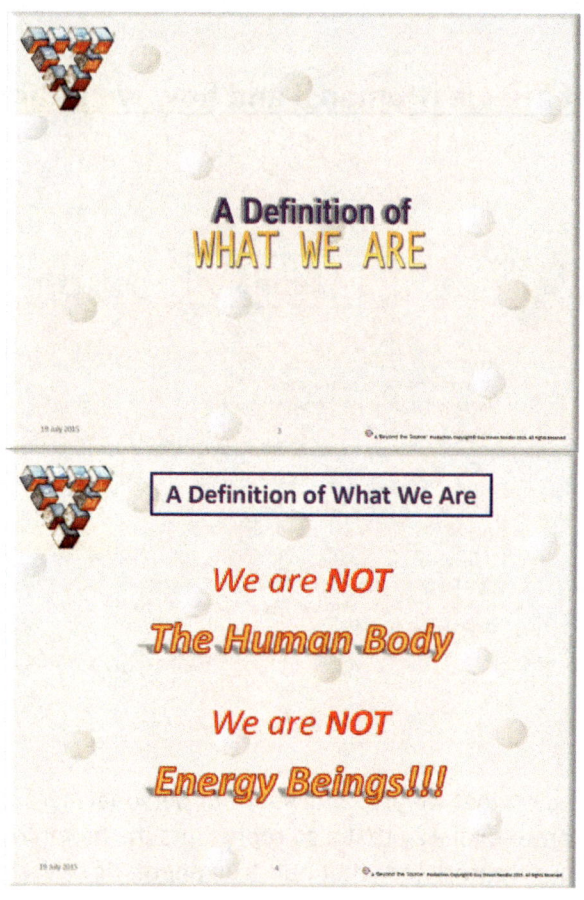

I think a lot of us think that we are energy beings, but we are not the human body or energy beings. So we may then be a bit confused about what we are. So to Guy's current level of understanding, which is transient, because as we move deeper into the knowledge base we move on with our understanding, and we are allowed to see more. We will also be going over some information we have covered previously, as it helps to get it to sink in and understand it better.

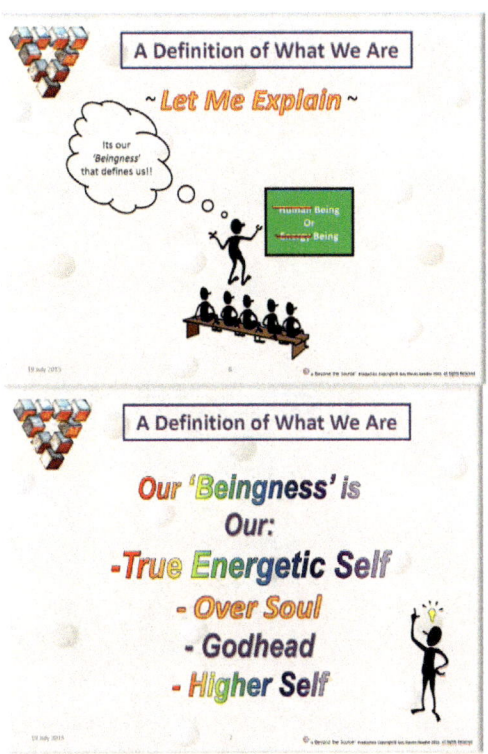

It is our *'beingness'* that defines who and what we are, and this *beingness* is our 'true energetic self', which guy says is not an exact representation of who we actually are, as the word énergetic' is a bit of a red herring, but he was told to use it at the beginning to help people to understand.

The true energetic self is the same as the óversoul'' (Dolores canon) or 'godhead' (Hindu religion) or 'higher self' (western world). If it's all these things, then what is the 'true energetic self'? It is, and we are **'Pure sentience'.** Consciousness, self awareness and conscious creativity etc are all things that are functions of what we are, consciousness for example is a part of the road that energy will go through in order to reach 'Pure sentience' but more than that, we are sentience that is 'given' a body of energy.

(A 'beyond the source production'.copyright © Guy Steven Needler. All rights reserved)

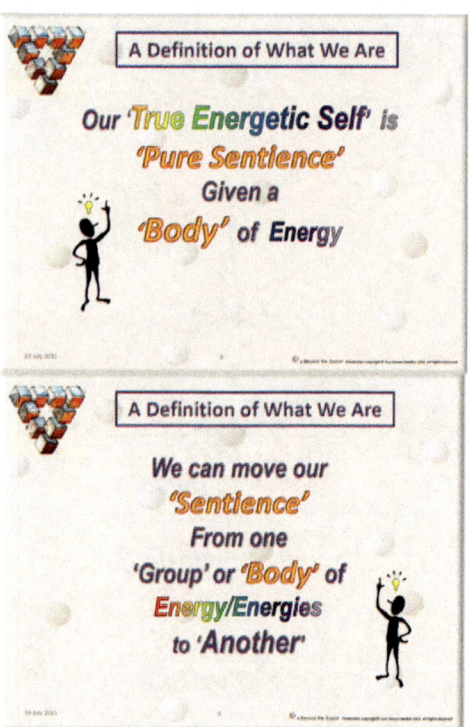

A body of energy is a vehicle that we use to house the sentience, it is how we move around in the environment that we use to evolve through, that part of the source which is being used for us, to help it evolve through.

We can move that sentience from one group or body to another, when we understand who and what we are and how we can work with those energies, we can move around. So the body of energy that we were given by our creator, the source, when we evolve to a point of understanding of what we are, we can move that sentience away from that original body of energies (or sphere of energy if you prefer) to anywhere around the source, and anywhere around the Multiversal environment that is given us to work with, and we can therefore relocate our sentience. And we do so, and actually even our source entity will do so as well. As our 'source entity' (God) is a creation of what is called 'The Origin', which is what the Hindu religion calls 'The Absolute', But that is another subject that I will tackle later on.

So we are pure sentience, pure sentience understands what it creates, perfects that creation and reproduces it. And it keeps going and sees where it can use its level of creativity to advance its own evolutionary progression. Progression is above evolution, evolution is just one part of what we do as we progress. One of the ways in which we use our sentience is to experience different environments which our true energetic self desires to accelerate its own evolutionary progress. And it does this by incarnating, by experiencing the lower frequencies of the Multiversal environment in a most profoundly integrated and immersed way, to experience things it would never do normally. But there is a structure behind that, we have a hierarchical structure, this structure is sort of static, but it will work with parallel conditions. We don't exist in one reality we have multiple realities in which we can exist within.

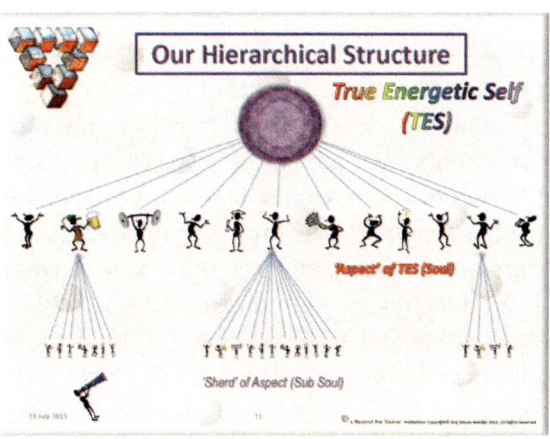

(A 'beyond the source production'.copyright © Guy Steven Needler. All rights reserved)

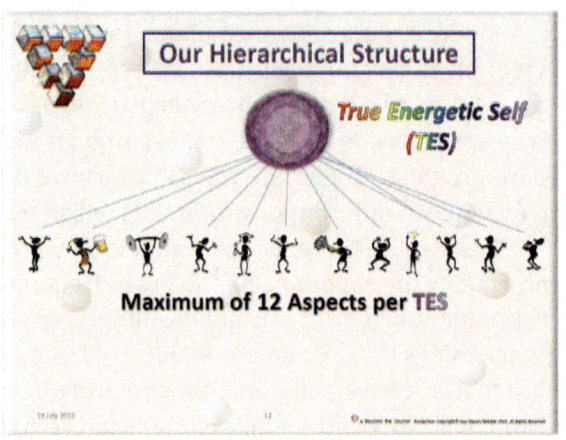

One of the ways which we do this in a static function, is to project parts of us, not us as human beings, but parts of our true energetic self. So we project parts out that become 'souls' or, they become 'sub souls'. You may notice that number 12 is increasingly seen in spiritual work, and you will see it here too. The reason behind it is because the number 12 proliferates itself in the structure of the Origin, which is copied down into the structure of the source and into ourselves, so what we can do in terms of our reproductability or our diversification of self is based upon 12. So we can in our higher self sense, in our true energetic self sense project a maximum of 12 'aspects' of ourselves. That is in our higher self sense, not in our 'soul' sense, as that is something that we as human beings use to associate ourselves with our 'spirit' and that is a bit limited in terms of what we really are.

So think of yourself as your 'higher self' right now, put yourself and your mind in your higher self's position, So you are not aspects or souls incarnate in the human body, you are now your higher self. Think of yourself as this much bigger ball of energy, this much larger aspect of individualised unit of sentience of the source. So there are 12 aspects that could be projected down from the true energetic self, out into very different Multiversal environments or universal environments, to experience different things in a parallel but linear condition.

(A 'beyond the source production'.copyright © Guy Steven Needler. All rights reserved)

The parallelisms occur when we have the opportunity to create a 'choice', a dualistic, trialistic, quadralistic choice. Where we have the possibility of possibilities or the possibility of possible possibilities to create other environments, through having a chance of going either this way, or that way, meeting this person here or conversely that person there and the different fractionalisation that can happen from that.

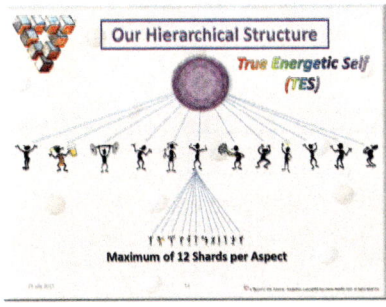 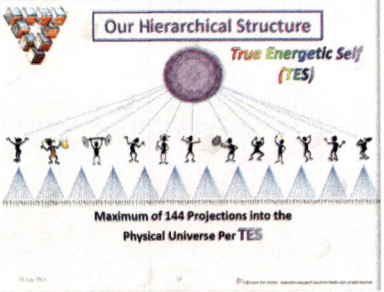

Now in general there is a percentage of sentience that remains in the energetic, 70% remains in the energetic, so if ourselves as true energetic selves projected all of our 12 aspects that we could project into the physical or other parts of the Multiversal environment were in fact projected, then 70% of us would remain in the energetic. The other 30% would spread out between those other 12 aspects or souls, which would mean that there is only about 2.5% of our sentience per soul.

As souls or aspects we are particularly powerful we are massive creators, so we can ourselves project 12 smaller versions of ourselves, 12 sub souls, or shards, again out into the physical or Multiversal environment. But, as with the true energetic self, we must retain 70% of our own sentience, so if we projected down 12 shards of our aspect or soul then each of those shards would have 2.5% of 2.5% of the sentience. So in effect if everything is projected out in a linear fashion there can be 144 projections from our higher self.

(A 'beyond the source production'.copyright © Guy Steven Needler. All rights reserved)

All of these things are concurrently understood, the memories, actions, emotions, behaviour, beingness, words, thoughts and experiences are

all concurrently absorbed by us as the true energetic self.

This makes you think and gives you a glimpse of how big we really are what we really are and how we really work.

The structure whilst we incarnate

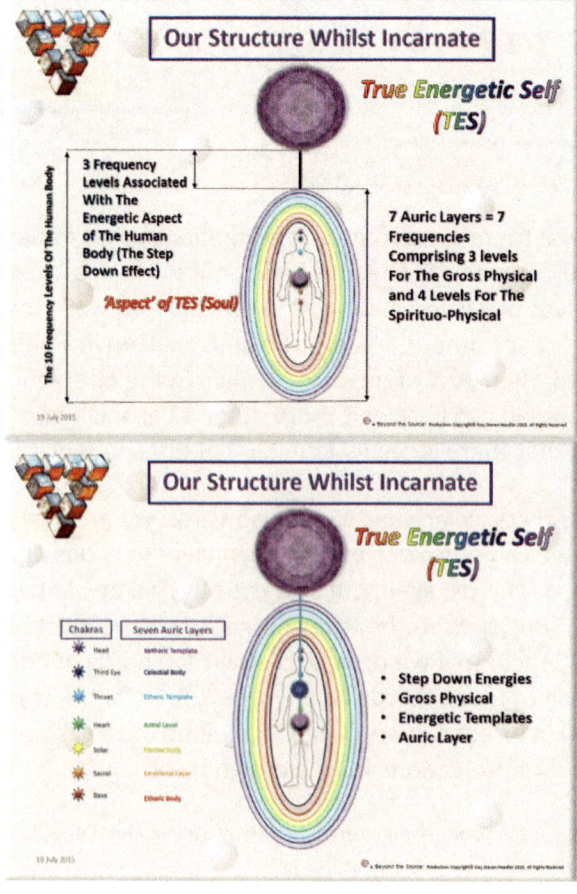

The process of incarnation is quite complex, simply put a small part of the sentient energy that is part of our TES (True Energetic Self) projects itself into a human body, an energy being that has a series of step down frequencies to experience this low environmental condition we call the physical universe. There are 10 frequencies associated with us, typically we know of 7 energy levels associated with the human form. Those energy levels comprise the requirement to create the human vehicle that we see right now. The first three create the gross physical, the next 4 create the physico-spiritual form, these are the essence of the vehicle that we use now, but there are also 3 other frequencies, and these are step down functions. These allow the energies that are a significantly higher frequency of where we are now from our TES to be funnelled down into the body that we call the human vehicle.

And so in essence there are 10 frequencies associated with the human form, the first 3 we don't really know about because we don't see them, there are no chakras or auric layers associated with them, there is no real connectivity associated with them that we as spiritual individuals on the path to being aware and awake would recognise, because they are too high a frequency. But when our TES decides to experience a low frequency environment it decides to do so in a way that is consistent with that low frequency environment. We experience resistance, pain, suffering, joy, delight, humour, birth, excitement, horror, pleasure etc and we do it by squeezing that little part of that sentience into this body. And the way it does that is by projecting this cord of energy which is called the 'Hara line' and the hara line goes down from the TES right down through the energy system to the zero point which is called the 'Tan tien' the tan tien exists, sort of, 3 inches above the naval and 3 inches into the centre of the body close to the spine. Around this point is where the solar plexus is, where all the chakras join up and spread out and are there to receive energy to maintain animation, like the battery or mains power for the physical form to work. When the essence of what we are comes down the hara line it stops at tan tien and anchors itself, it then goes up to where the heart chakras (front and back) join the hara line. And it then creates another area called the 'soul seat', this is the essence of what we are. The 'soul seat' is the essence of where we are, and it is just behind the sternum. And from there the energy associated with the control of the human form spreads out and we get the meridian lines that go to the chakras the minor chakras, and the ability for the soul or the aspect to animate the body. Then the ability to experience this environment through the body is achieved.

How we incarnate

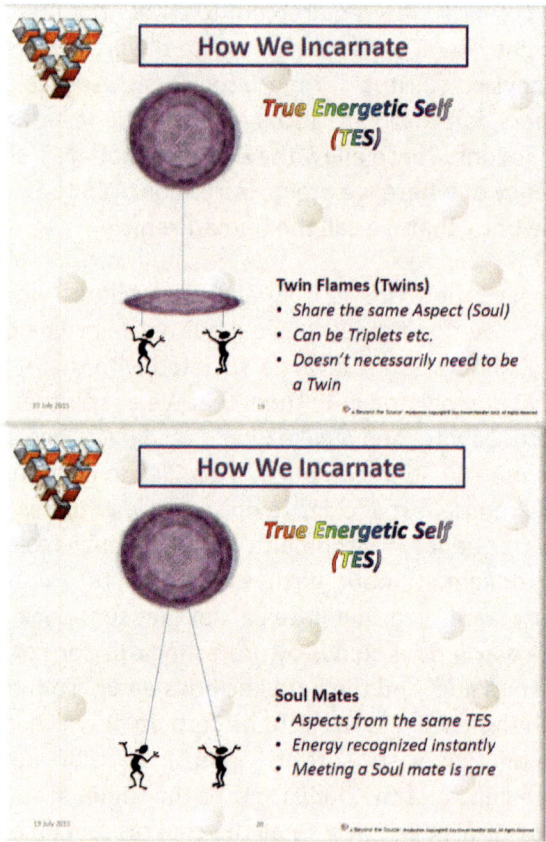

Twin flames: One of the ways in which we incarnate is known as 'twin flames' which is a sharing of the same soul (aspect) between two bodies, it has nothing to do with being a soul mate. It is usually a function of being twins at the embryo stage of gestation, where the soul can very easily go into those two bodies and grow together. Sometimes that soul can be split into three and become triplets, although we don't tend to see the triplets functioning in the same way as we see twins do, there may be one that is different.

That does not mean that that soul needs to function in the same way, and so a soul can split itself into various different parts, outside of being a shard, and take itself into different bodies that are not necessarily in the same womb. So when we see someone that is a twin flame, it does not mean that they are born from the same mother, it can be different mothers. So it would not be the same thought process as you would see from those that are born as twins from the same mother.

Soul mates: Soul mates are aspects that are generated from the same TES. So soul mates are part of a 'soul group' and a soul group is a function of all the aspects or souls projected from the same TES. Soul mates are interesting because we know we have a soul mate the moment we see one, they don't just communicate with language or bodies, and they communicate energetically all the time. So when you meet a soul mate, it is extremely profound, you know each other on a deep level and can know each other's thoughts. It is also extremely rare to meet a soul mate, because there are only 12 of them in the whole of the multiverse potentially. So to find a true soul mate is extremely difficult, so when you think you have met your soul mate, it might be something else. It might be a twin flame or a 'sympathetic soul'.

(A 'beyond the source production'.copyright © Guy Steven Needler. All rights reserved)

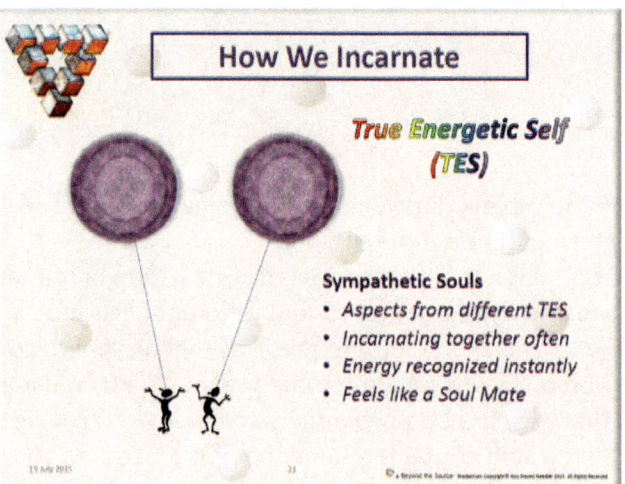

Sympathetic soul: is a soul that is interacting with another soul or aspect from a different TES and they do it on a regular basis, they do it often. Again the energy is recognised instantly, it's there all of the time and it feels like a soul mate. And so you should do, you know this energy, this person, this soul, it's part of what you are to recognise energy as you work with these things all the time it's just that we don't know what we are dealing with sometimes and don't know how to describe it.

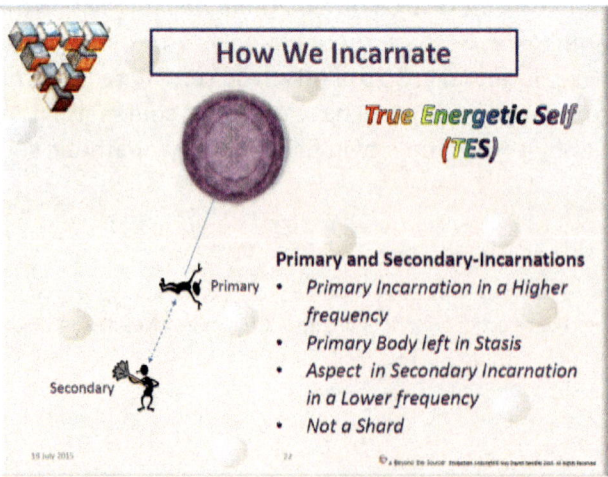

Secondary-incarnation: Now things start to get interesting, we can have something that is a 'primary' incarnation that can have a 'secondary'

incarnation. So we can incarnate, and then have an incarnation 'within' an incarnation, this incarnation is not a parallel incarnation, it is a linear incarnation. But there still is the possibility of different realities that are created through the different choices we make. Dualities, tri-realities, quadrualities the possibility of possibilities and possibility of those possibilities being possible. And the fractualised parallel environments that we create.

But this is fairly static, this when an entity, or aspect decides to incarnate in a higher frequency vehicle, a higher frequency body a body that is still incarnate as a vehicle but is at a higher frequency within the structure of the physical universe, in a frequency so high that we would consider it energetic. We experience it a lot sometimes, as we see craft come and go, we see individuals appear in from of our faces and then disappear. But the aspect or soul that incarnates in a vehicle, a body that is higher than where we are now is able to have the functionality associated with that frequency and so above a certain level a soul or aspect is fully aware, fully capable of everything that it can do when it is in the disincarnate state whilst being incarnate. As a result of that it can decide to leave that body to leave it behind to leave it in stasis and then move out into a different form to enjoy an incarnation that may take several years from our perspective and then feedback that information to its primary incarnate state. Sometimes that body is still maintained, and sometimes that body is still active and the soul travels backwards and forwards between the primary and secondary incarnate vehicle. That can cause some confusion sometimes because sometimes the memories leak between the two. There are some interesting phenomena with this because it can cause disorientation. And in my case I had memories of being a different person in a different place, with blonde hair, with others that also had blonde hair, which as a child I just thought they were dreams, but now I recognise that they were memories leaking through.

(A 'beyond the source production'.copyright © Guy Steven Needler. All rights reserved

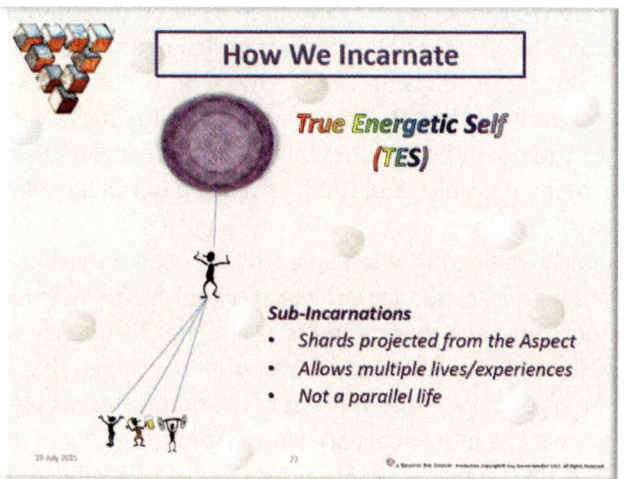

Sub-incarnations: a sub-incarnation is a definition of what a shard is, it is *not* a real incarnation, it's a way in which we can experience things in a 'multiple condition' note, not a parallel, but a multiple-condition. It allows us to experience many lives and get those experiences and feed them back in into the aspect. So some us may think that we are experiencing many lives concurrently. Are you wondering if you are a shard? Well, you won't be if you are reading this, as shards do not have the sentient capacity to understand or be interested in this kind of information. Sometimes the shards will be in the same environment as the aspect, sometime they will be in different parts of the physical universe. But it is not a parallel life, it is a linear concurrent life, when the shard dies, it does not retain any individuality but is just re-absorbed back into the aspect.

(A 'beyond the source production'.copyright © Guy Steven Needler. All rights reserved

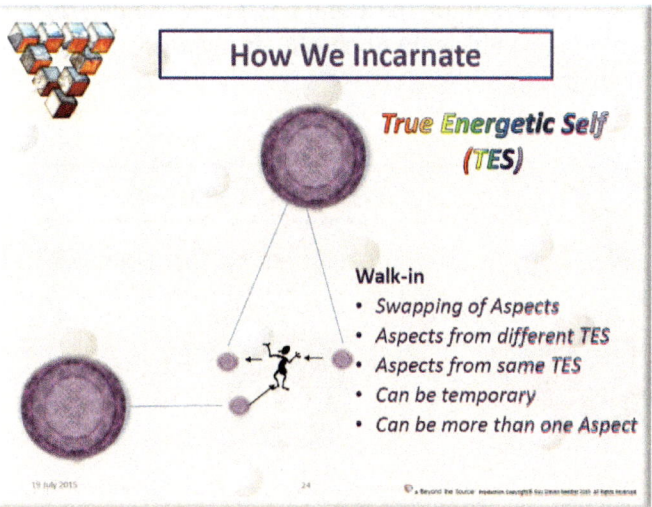

Walk-ins: Is the swapping out of aspects into a body, sometimes souls don't want to do a whole incarnation, they only want to do a certain part of that incarnation. Maybe it's the birth process; maybe it is when the person is experiencing adolescence, adulthood, the demise process. Sometimes a single body can be used as a single vehicle for many souls, so they can swap in and out. That is when sometimes you can see somebody change overnight, the memory of the previous existence is maintained by the new soul entering, and sometimes the energy is not quite right in terms of the individual from the human perspective who interfaces with that new soul, so perhaps what we have is that people think "oh, such and such has changed suddenly, they use to be a nice person, and now they are not" for example, and this is because the soul has changed. There could be many walk-ins in the body in a lifetime of that vehicle, it doesn't have to be just one. It can also be temporary, so that the soul moves out of the body, go and do something else and another soul comes in just to have a certain experience, and then move out again so the first soul or primary soul can come back in. There can also be more than one soul or aspect in a body at the same time, sometimes there can be a primary soul animating the body and another soul may want to experience the incarnate experience, but not be particularly interested in animating the body, interacting with people and working things out, taking on board responsibility, evolving, doing things. And so they will 'piggy-back' so to speak, they will go into the body but become a kind of 'back seat passenger', seeing through the eyes of the human vehicle, but not influencing what is going on, this apparently happens quite a lot.

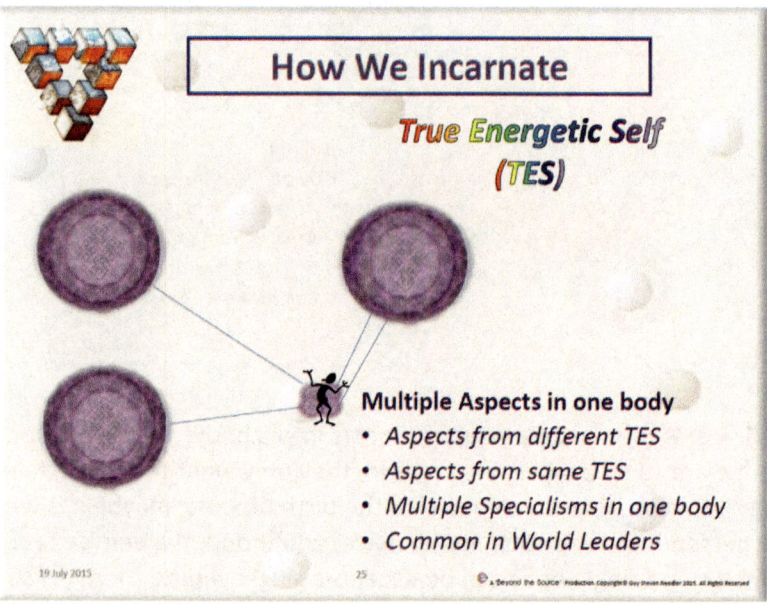

Multiple souls in a body at the same time: We have or need to have multiple souls in the same body, when there is a significant piece of work that needs to be done. Those souls can be from the same TES or from different TES's it is common it is common for people to are going to have a world or galactic significance to have more than one soul in the same body. There need to be different specialism's, different experiences or different knowledge bases that are not normally available to a soul via 'taking a download' for instance from the 'akashic records'. Each of these souls are allowed to drive the body at certain points, certain specialism's used by certain souls to interface with certain environments. It is quite common for world leaders to have more than one soul associated with their physical form.

((A 'beyond the source production'.copyright © Guy Steven Needler. All rights reserved)

How we incarnate affects us psychologically

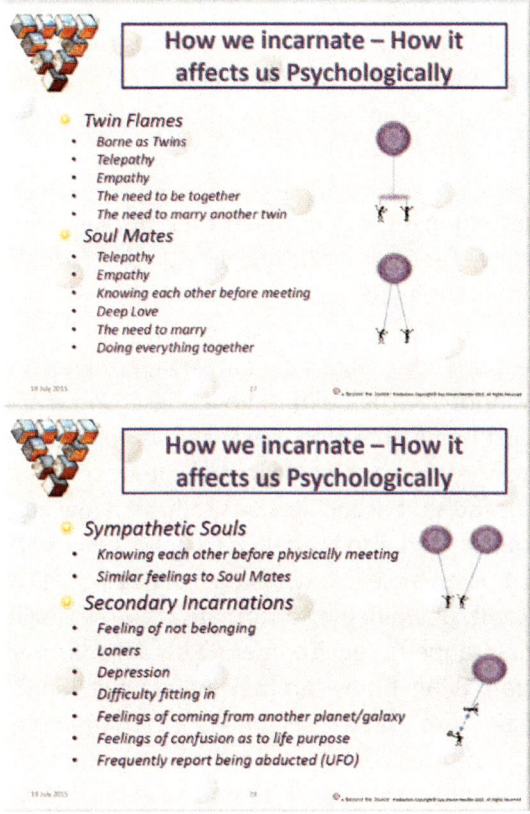

Twin flames: They are acting as one, because they are one, two different vehicles, but the same soul, Or even 3 or 4 vehicles sometimes.

Soul mates: They almost operate in the same way as twin flames, they have telepathy and empathy, and they know each other before meeting. Soul mates experience profound love for each other never apart, doing everything together. Neither can do any wrong, they always forgive each other.

(A 'beyond the source production'.copyright © Guy Steven Needler. All rights reserved

Sympathetic souls: These as well as the previous two operate very similarly, as they are used to working together. Similar feelings, empathy and other levels of communication, desires, wants, needs, behaviours, actions and thoughts.

Secondary Incarnations: These have left their primary soul in a different location, they have feelings of not really belonging here, they are mostly loners, sometimes suffer severe depression and have difficulty in fitting in. They can have a lot of feelings of coming from different planets or galaxies. Can experience feelings of confusion, not knowing why they are here and cannot see the point of being here. Some of them frequently report being abducted, because their primary incarnation is at a level where that primary incarnate vehicle travels around the galaxy or the universe, and that aspect decides to have a low incarnate physical experience, and also that all of its colleagues will benefit from that experience. Then once in a while the colleagues will take the body away to monitor it, downloading information and seeing how it is coping in its low frequency environment with a higher frequency aspect/soul. Identifying if they can they maintain its longevity for long enough and make sure that the secondary incarnation is efficient and is being used to its optimal condition. So it would be quite regular for medical examinations to happen with these people who are experiencing secondary incarnations, specifically if they are providing lots of information and data about their environment back to where the primary incarnation is residing.

(A 'beyond the source production'.copyright © Guy Steven Needler. All rights reserved

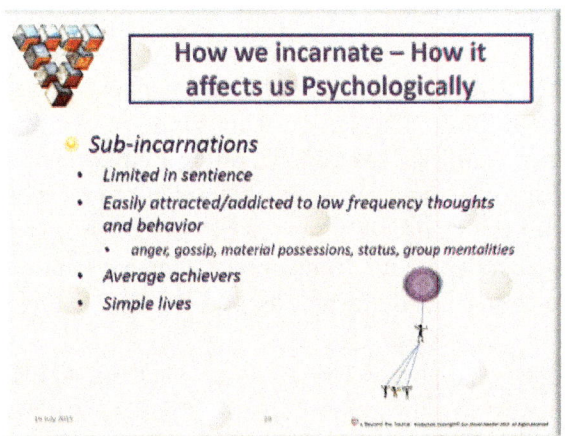

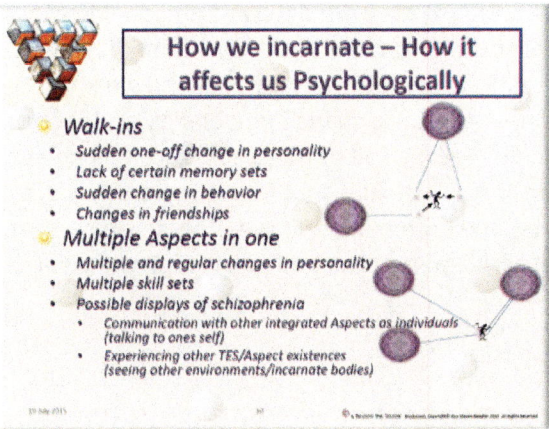

<u>Sub-incarnations</u>: Remember the level of sentience of the shards from before, 2.5% of 2.5% that comes from the TES. So these individuals are particularly attracted to material existence. They are limited in their thought processes in how they interact with others and they are easily attracted to low frequency behaviour patterns, thoughts, actions, desires and wants, and the way they behave is particularly relevant to what they are from a sentient level perspective. They constantly indulge in gossip, they desire and crave material possessions, they want to have status and they tend to have group mentalities where they coalesce together where individuals are indulging in low frequency thought processes or actions and behaviours, they are easily attracted to a crowd who are angry. In general they will be average achievers at best

and will have simple lives.

Walk-ins: Lots of these people have one-off changes in personality, also people who might have lost their memory for no reason at all, or that the memory set changes, like suddenly not remembering people they have known for many years, and has different set of memories as a different existence in a different part of the world. They might have sudden changes in behaviour, if they are staying for a considerable time you will find a change in friendships as well.

Multiple aspects in one body: These people will have regular changes in personality, almost like they have psychosis, like you are speaking to different individuals, different personalities in the same body. Schizophrenia, because they are different personalities in the same body, different souls all in the same body, some of these things will talk to each other as well, sometimes they could be walking down the road talking to themselves, it will change personality and then talk to themselves again. Because all of these souls are talking at the same time, but there is no particular soul that is the dominant soul. There should really be one dominant, and the others as back seat passengers just observing and experiencing and not driving the vehicle.

This was just a snapshot of some ways we can incarnate; there are apparently many other ways.

(A 'beyond the source production'.copyright © Guy Steven Needler. All rights reserved)

Diary of continuing experiences and understanding

Dream visions

I have had many dream visions, showing and telling me information about my real self, others I know in my primary incarnation and also information about space and other dimensional and frequency facts. One such vision was of the nature of space and life in it. This was in **2019**, I saw three glowing entities in space, they had a white glow that had a blue tinge to it, the light radiated out in the surrounding space, but I could still see the stars in the background, there was no 'hard' edge to the light. Also although there seemed to me to be three, they were conjoined in some way. They had an inner part that had a roundish formation but was not exactly round only approximating roundness, and then within that round part were white 'orbs' of light and also long 'ribbon' looking things, that were like flat ribbons, that twisted and turned. It was these 'ribbons' that stretched between the three entities, showing that they were connected in some way together. I was fascinated by these entities, they looked interesting and beautiful, had a warm friendly feeling to them. Then my vision started to go 'down' from them, showing structures in space. These structures were built one on top of another, and also to the sides, filling the whole of 'space' as my vision was continuing downwards. They were in a round shape, the colour of a kind of red/ brown that reminds me of earthenware like they were made of dried mud or something. Some had a section that protruded from the middle of the round doughnut like cylindrical shape, and that protruding part was yellow. Above the yellow protruding part were 'windows' or porthole like looking openings, which had a bright yellow light, shining through them. I was getting feelings along with the vision, and it was that these were all 'homes' to beings, all the homes were connected and continued down to what eventually was a flat ground, that I 'knew' was representing 'Planet Earth'. And then I got the intuitive message that all of space, right down to our planet, was absolutely choc-a-block full of life, there was absolutely no part of space that did not contain life, so that the purpose of the universe was to have life, not that life is perhaps an anomaly, as science would have you believe, but the complete opposite. Life is ubiquitous and indeed the purpose. It was a beautiful message and confirmatory, as this is what I had believed to be the case for many years. I don't know who the 'three' beings were or represented, but they were the ones giving the message, I did my best to reproduce the vision in drawings below.

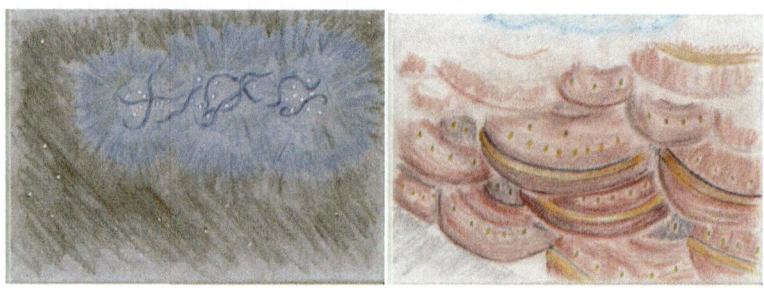

The three 'beings' - Life filling space beneath the three beings

11/09/2021 I received information whilst sleeping, that I am married, to a younger wife, that her name is 'Noreaga', her name was said to me very purposefully, it was said 3 times in a row, and each time the name Noreaga was said, it was said louder and with more emphasis. This was to make sure that I would remember her name. Also the voice said (Could have been my own voice, my primary incarnation) that Noreaga has 'special abilities', it also said that I was avoiding her initially when I first met her, it didn't specify why I was avoiding her though, and that also she can find me wherever I am. I call her 'Norri' for short I'm guessing I might do that as well when back in my primary incarnation where we live, but I don't know that for sure.

14/09/2021
I was talking to my friend Ruth, who has a great ability to tune into beings from all levels of existence, and I told her about my experience of finding out I have a wife. This revelation was pretty wild for me, it took a little getting my head around, but when talking to Ruth I remembered a dream, that I now think was a partial memory relating some truths to me. I think this dream might have been in **2018** or perhaps later after

meeting myself, the primary incarnation. In this 'dream' I was walking along a path outside with a lady, and we were approaching a large entranceway to what I considered to be a 'park' of some sort. Then as we approached the entrance a 'female' ran off in front of me and went to a 'stall' of some sort, the details of which I didn't make out, but I think may have been a food or game stall? I was relaying this memory to Ruth, and when I said this part, she suddenly said "oh, that's your daughter!" which was another shocking revelation. It did however make sense to me, the female running past to the stall was a lot shorter than me, and it felt right, it just clicked in my mind, so it all made sense! This park was like a theme park, with rides etc. I think at this point the dream changed slightly, although still in the park it was telling me another story. As the lady who I was walking with, whom I now recognise was Norri, went over to a ride, rather like a big wheel, with pods, something like the London eye. And I could now see Norri sitting in the lowest pod next to the window. As I looked at her, she was sitting with her head facing down slightly and looking at me sideways, not looking particularly happy. This also was making me feel rather sad, and I wondered why she was there without me? I believe this was an analogy of me being here in this place/ lower frequency existence and she was on the ship. I thought 'oh well, I don't know what I can do about it, as she is there and I am here'. So I started to walk on and walked past where I could see her in the ride, towards the back of the ride, where I hoped I could find a way in to be with her. Then as I was walking along, Norri came out of the ride, through a door, I was very happy that she had come to see me, I went towards her and we held hands. There was something odd about it though, as I was holding her hand I realised that I was a lot shorter than her now, and I could just see up to her chest height, I noticed that she was wearing a white top, which was tight fitting and I could see the outline of her breasts, but I could not see any higher. I feel that this represents when she came to see me when I was much younger in my teenage years, I think after I saw the UFO. I have a memory of seeing someone standing in the road at the end of the Lane where I use to live. It was a dead end lane with common land that went for miles; it was in fact the exact place where I saw the UFO in the sky after I had the close encounter. I was always confused as to whether this was a real event or a dream, as it felt so real, but I can't remember exactly when it was. This lady who was standing there reminded me of a girl I knew at primary school, and I thought for years that it was her standing there, and in the memory a friend I was with said "she is waiting for you, aren't you going to go over and see her?" to which I felt a bit nervous and shy about. But after all of these revelations about being married, I now recognise that it was Norri, as I drew this event on paper and when drawing it the lady in the road was wearing an all in one white jumpsuit and had the same Facial features and hair. And when I look back after realising this, I recognise that Norri has been with me my whole life, appearing in dreams. She always looks the same, she is a Caucasian lady with black hair in a 'bob' and is attractive and seems tall and slim. So the reason I could only see up to her chest was, in my mind, because it was from my early teens when I was 12 to 15 perhaps and not so tall, although I suspect she is taller than my earthly body even now, I'm not so tall at 5ft 7in, but I think she is much taller. So this was the beginning of recognising that Norri has been with me my whole life. Even the giant spider dream if you remember from earlier, that was Norri's head and body, she really has been with me in many ways, I am blown away by it all.

Norri (Noreaga) standing at the end of the lane in white jumpsuit

Meditation Late September 2021 Whilst in meditation I heard a voice say " A telecommunications analyst" there was no reference to whom that might be, but I took it as what Norri's main job is on board a ship I presume, of course apart from being mum to our daughter, whose age I have no idea about at this point.

October 2021 I decided to try and draw my primary incarnation as I remembered him, so I set pencil to paper. But as I was drawing him, I suddenly realised I was drawing him in 'blue'. This was not conscious, but obviously unconscious control by my primary self. So apparently I am a 'Blue being' I put the picture below, this was another amazing 'realisation', so not only am I this being with a whole life in another frequency within the universe, but I am more influenced by him than I realised as I am now drawing him in the correct skin colour.

Primary incarnation in a 'Blue' skin tone

Dream state late November 2021 In this experience I was sitting across a table from Norri, she looked the same as before but I remember more of how her face looked this time, very attractive, cute and she was very smiley. I had three questions for her, of which I can't remember what they were now. Norri telepathically knew the questions that I had for her and answered them before I could barely bring them to thought, let alone speak them out verbally. I was very impressed and a bit surprised, as I was not expecting that. We were holding hands across the table and I could feel an amazing amount of love coming from her, and I could also feel the love welling up inside me and pouring out. It was an amazing experience, and one I try to hold on to the most, although the feeling is hard to bring up now I can still remember how I wanted to describe it. One thing I remember is that whilst holding hands I could see a bit of her forearms sticking out from under the sleeves of her top, they were not in focus as I was concentrating on her face and feelings and emotions there, but I noticed that her forearms looked like they had some pink spots, much more than that I can't say, but it was a very memorable and lovely experience.

Norri as I remember her holding hands across a table

Mid December 2021 I was meditating late one night about 1am in the morning. It was a really good, grounded meditation I felt myself going quite deep. After finishing the meditation being quite tired I went straight to bed. As soon as my head hit the pillow it was like I 'fell' through the pillow into another place. I was completely conscious and aware. It was not like a lucid dream, it was 'real', I found myself in a dark place in which I could not see anything at first, then I looked slightly down and to my left and I saw a 'panel'. It was dimly lit by the numbers and letters on the buttons and a dim light defining its shape. As I was examining this panel I heard myself saying "oh there is another being here with me?" and then 'I' said "oh, hello there". Then as soon as I got there I was suddenly back in my bed, awake. So I started to think about and analyse what happened, I am pretty sure that I was in the 'immersion pod' wherever my primary incarnations body is and the panel was some control unit for the pod. What appears to me to have happened next is my primary incarnation realised that the consciousness from this secondary incarnation had gone back to the primary, but, that the primary was also consciously aware. So the primary said 'oh I think there is another being here' and also the friendly 'Hello there' to me, the secondary incarnation. So clearly, it is possible to split your consciousness, at that level of frequency anyway, and be living and having two conscious, consciousnesses in the same place, at the same time, in the same body! Wow!

So I drew the panel that I saw but when I went to put the numbers and letters on the buttons, I couldn't do it I only saw squiggles and dots in my mind, I have replicated it as well as I could, but I don't know how accurate, if at all the squiggles are. So when in the pod in the primary incarnations mind I understood the language, and translated it into English letters and numerals, such a complex experience. I told Guy Needler about this episode and sent him the picture to see what he made of it.

Guys reply regarding the panel *"It was a form of written communication, a powerful one that has energetic information embedded within it. The Egyptians had something similar"*.

And this was guys response to being two consciousnesses at the same time, place, and body *"Yes that happens, Sentience is much more powerful than what the expectations of brain function will ever be"*. So that was an interesting and amazing response, he saw the power in the symbols and recognised they had energy within them; he also appears to have heard or is aware of the power of having two consciousnesses in the same place etc. I don't think I will ever stop learning about the possibilities of reality and of being a sentient consciousness in this universe, and of being amazed.

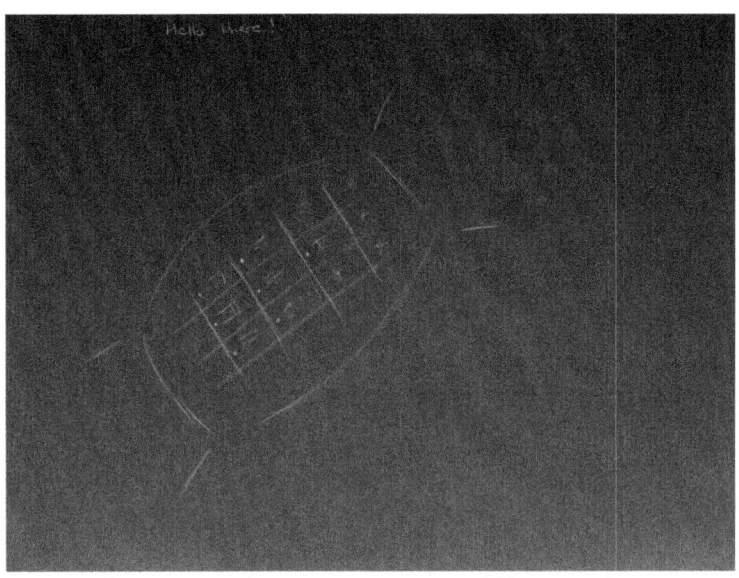

Immersion Pod panel with the powerful language

Late December 2021 This was a vivid dream, I was in a building, but I realise that it could have been a ship I was walking around, I walked into a room to see a female sleeping on a bed, I sat on the edge of the bed and leaned over to kiss her on the side of the forehead, she was facing away from me so I didn't see her face, I think she had long dark hair. I found that a bit odd, as I was more of a watcher than a participant in this dream, although it was vivid. Then I got up and started to wander around and I thought let's see who else is here and check out some more rooms. And that is where the dream ended. I realised after, that when I thought about the female sleeping in the bed, I thought of my friend Ruth's daughter, which made me realise, that this was 'my' daughter asleep in bed. So this was more of a memory seeing it through the eyes of the primary incarnation, although some of the physical aspects were changed, for instance I believe my daughter has blonde hair, not black, so the details of the living space may also not be exactly as it is in reality. I think it is memories leaking through from my primary incarnation as Guy has expounded in his information regarding secondary incarnations, but I feel this is more proof that I do have a daughter. I also believe her name may be Nirri.

Early January 2022 I remembered this 'dream' or 'out of body' experience recently. I had gone to bed, I presume I drifted off to sleep, but suddenly found myself, at night, standing naked (I sleep naked in bed) in front of, and looking out of, my bedroom window. Then I started to move forwards passing seamlessly through the wall and window to hover for a moment or two outside. I am on the first floor so this would be roughly 3 meters from the ground outside. And then I felt this 'pull' and started to float upwards towards the over-laden clouds, it must have been a night where the moon was bright as I could see some light between the layers of cloud. I was starting to feel a bit panicky as I was being pulled up towards an unknown destination, but I said in my mind, "no, don't worry, and just go with it". Then I think I started to speed up in my movement towards the clouds, but as that started to happen, I went blank. The next thing I know I am in bed with my eyes closed, remembering what happened in the encounter before blanking out. I jumped out of bed and went to the window and opened the curtains. The sky looked just like I had just seen it in my experience, I was hoping I would see a craft briefly or some indication of who was taking me, but unfortunately not, and there was nothing except clouds that I could see. I was very conscious and aware in this event and so I believe it could have taken place either in this physical reality or it could have been an out of body kind of experience (OBE). I think this was probably one of the times my colleagues had taken me for downloading information etc, although my memory has been blocked of what happened on the craft. I think they wanted me to remember leaving so that it would be more conformation of what Guy had said about what happens to secondary incarnations.

19/01/2022
I started to read one of Guy Needler's books "The Origin speaks", I have owned it since 2018 after conversing with Guy by email, I only looked at parts that I thought were interesting. This time, I thought I would start from the beginning. I should start by trying briefly to explain what 'The Origin' is in Guy's experience and understanding. Guy has communicated through meditation and channelling, entities that make up the universe eventually talking directly to what he calls 'source entity one'. This is what is referred to as 'God' in the Abrahamic traditions around the world. There are according to Guy 12 such source entities,

each with their own multiverses doing things in different ways. These 12 'Source entities' were created by what guy calls 'The Origin' which is the ultimate creator in Guys understanding. I am not here to question that, although what created the ultimate creator is what comes to my mind, but the Origin is already beyond my comprehension, so I think for now I will leave it there. On the very first page of chapter 1 Guy described the arrival of the Origin to begin the channelled work for that book *"I felt the Origin, its energies cool like a cold shower came over me, and we commenced dialogue."* This short statement piqued my interest as I recalled two incidences that reminded me of what Guy just said. The first incident was at Amaravati Buddhist monastery in Hertfordshire UK where I ordained as a monk. This was before I ordained, but I was staying there as a lay resident. I was in my room with a friend I had made there, Juan a Spanish man who was visiting and staying as a guest also. I was reading some passage from the Pali cannon, which is a collection of scriptures in the Theravada Buddhist tradition, and after finishing reading the passage I stopped and paused, the air was still, it was silent with us both taking in the meaning of what was said, I felt it deeply and then I felt this cool wind blow 'through' me, in a still room with no movement or wind. I didn't feel the cool wind on my skin, but it literally was felt like it blew right through my body and mind. My friend Juan is a very sensitive empathic, and feels everything going on around him. And just after I felt that cool breeze, he turned around suddenly and looked at me, his mouth agape and I said "did you feel that?" he nodded in amazement. Whether Juan felt that independently or just through me, I don't know, as I was unaware of his abilities at that time, I just thought that we both had a shared experience. The second incident I was visiting Cittaviveka Buddhist monastery in Hampshire UK, a sister monastery to Amaravati, I was with another friend Josh, we sat on a bench in the beautiful grounds just soaking up the quiet stillness and again I felt the same cool breeze blow through me, not 'ON' me. It was also a still day, I said to josh "did you feel that, It was like a cool breeze" he seemed to agree, but I don't know if he really felt it or not, I just assumed he did.

So on reading Guys passage about a cool shower, I suddenly recalled the events from about 20 years previously, I had to write to Guy again and ask him about his experience and explained my two previous experiences. Guy replied

"*Thank you for contacting me and sharing your experiences. I can say that you have certainly felt the energy of The Origin through the book. Quite a few people, who are sensitive enough, do. That is the extremely subtle side of its energies, noting of course that, ultimately, we are part of its sentience, albeit, significantly small in an incomparable way. If one is sensitive enough one can feel such energies in Buddhist and higher quality (the monks that is) Hindu temples and I experienced the same whilst listening to a group of monks chanting "Om" in a monastery temple in Japan".*

So not that I am 'communicating' with the Origin, but that I was able to feel its energies, what a privilege I feel that was and is very interesting, also adding to my belief in Guys experience and understanding of the structure of the universe and the beings in it as he has understood it.

Pleiadians and other ET beings

Meditation 03/02/2022 I was having the feeling of energy moving around the 3rd eye, I haven't felt that since meditating at the monastery nearly 20 years ago. Whilst meditating I had some images shooting past my inner eye. One of the images 'took centre stage' in my consciousness, it was an image of a Lions head, he was looking ahead of himself, but not directly at me, I was looking at him from his left hand side. I 'felt' that he was sitting on a seat, his back upright. He was very well groomed he had large Green eyes and looked very thoughtful. I wasn't shocked to see him, or frightened in any way. Quite the opposite, I felt he looked familiar, I felt comfortable with his presence. I believe he is one of the feline Lion beings, I have heard of their existence, but this is the first time I have 'seen' one, as a human, although only in this meditational state. I could only see just his head, but I could make out that there was some dark clothing around his neck line, but I could not see more detail.

I talked with Ruth about this vision and she was able to contact him, apparently his name is 'Raani' and you could imagine him rolling out the 'R's and extending the 'A's in a kind of understated roaring. Apparently Raani and I are good friends and he thinks of me as a 'brother', I can actually feel like I feel the same about him when I conjure up the image of him that I saw. I have seen videos from the 'Cosmic Agency' (CA) channel on YouTube, they have talked about Lion beings, they called them the 'Urmah' I am not sure if he is from the same particular race, I think there are quite a few different groups, although that is just my speculation. But CA have said that the lions are one of the most ancient races in this universe, they are very fierce and one of the most feared in battle, but that they are a positive race now. And also that they can speak but it is easier for them to communicate telepathically, they are comrades of the Taygetan Pleiadians and work closely together. I was 'led' to the CA channel after meeting my primary incarnation in 2018, I believe that at least some information is genuinely reflecting some truths, whether the people on this channel are in genuine contact or not I cannot know, I just use my intuition and gut feeling about what sounds right, and what does not resonate with me. I believe the main reason for being led to the channel is that it was to give me understanding about some aspects of my newly expanding reality.

This brought up a memory of a dream I had a little while before this, I cannot remember if it was days or weeks or even a month or so before hand. I am not very good with remembering times and dates. I think it's because of my off planet connection and of having meetings with my star family, having memories suppressed etc its messed up my feeling of time, so now I try to write down the dates of memories, visions, meditations etc, part of the reason for writing all of this down now, so I have a record of a timeline when things have happened. Anyway, this dream/meeting I had went something like this.

I was walking along somewhere, with a man, I didn't really know him or recognise him, I don't recall what we were saying to each other, but at some point he disappeared behind me, then all of a sudden I felt these 'arms' going over the top of my shoulders, and pinning me, strongly so that I could not move. Then I heard this really loud, low rumbling growl, it was very powerful and was quite scary. I thought to myself, Oh shit I think I'm about to be chewed up by a reptilian being, as I have read and heard on videos many disturbing things regarding negative reptilians, although I believe there are also positive reptilians of a different faction, but anyway, I was afraid for a few seconds. But I then realised a few things: 1) I am not afraid of death because I had a near death experience when I was 21 that cured me of the fear of death, and also 2) I am an immortal multi dimensional being and ultimately cannot be killed, and 3) That nothing is real and only the creation of energy. So the reptilian beings who want to chew on you, to cause pain, suffering and fear, feed on this mixture, 'loosh' I think it's called, so it's not just about eating flesh it's the emotional and mental mixture of it all. I thought, well It might be able to give me pain, but I won't give it the fear, so I will be an empty victim, and the pain will be short lived before I die or move on. So I said "OK come on then" in a loud provocative and aggressive way. But then nothing happened? And after what seemed like quite a while the interaction and dream came to an end. I was talking to Ruth about this, this was before I saw and knew who Raani is. On pondering the meaning of the dream I had the thought that maybe it was a protective wolf putting its legs over my shoulders, as I had heard of that in shamanic descriptions. But Ruth said no, and thought it was a Lion. So I thought on that and yes, that felt right. So the rumbling growl was not a reptilian, but the growl of a lion, which I now believe is confirmed by learning of Raani. Wow, I can see how frightening it would be up against a Lion or a pack of lions. He was showing me that I am being protected by him and that was absolutely an awesome experience and I am very grateful for the protection and friendship that I feel we have together.

Ruth is now well connected to Raani, apparently we all know each other from before this human experience and came here on missions. Ruth has now got more information on what we are doing here and our connection to Raani and more. Apparently Raani is an ambassador for his race, he attends Galactic federation meetings and he knows me probably because I am apparently fairly high up in the hierarchy of my race. I think due to my experiences I have a more overall picture of what is going on and the mission of what Starseeds that I am connected with are doing here on Earth strategically, more than that I don't know, but I know I have the ability of seeing many steps ahead and planning the steps in a very quick time, and I guess I am a hands on type of being too, as I am here. My role I believe at this present time on Earth is as a Data gatherer, I get data from people, through telepathic means, but I am not always or generally aware of doing it. Also by listening to others through social media, the alternative media and alternative groups, assessing the data including feelings and emotions of the general public etc. This feeling of 'data gathering' fits in with Guys explanation of the purpose of a 'secondary incarnation' as that is a good description for part of my reason for being here. I feel I do a lot of things whilst my human body is asleep, but I generally don't have any memory of what I was doing, but it probably does explain why sometimes I feel tired after sleeping. This all sounds completely 'out there', even for me, and perhaps my stance will change with more experiences and knowledge, but this is where I am right now. I treat all information and ideas that are not a direct experience of myself purely as 'information', I neither take it to heart as absolute truth nor 'throw the baby out with the bathwater' as the saying goes. I just hold it outside of myself, and as more direct experience and information that I trust comes to me, these parcels of 'information' either get closer to me, or further away.

A fair representation of Raani, the Maine is good although his real face is much more handsome and his eyes are larger.

February 10th 2022 Dream vision – I was talking with some people, I believe they may all have been ladies. I distinctly remember 'looking down' on them physically clearly showing that I am a lot taller than they are, we were in a hallway and appear to have stopped as we bumped into each other. Then for some reason I said to them "No hablo Espanol" which is Spanish for "I Don't speak Spanish" I was finding it quite difficult to physically speak this, but I managed to, even though it was a struggle with my mouth and vocal chords (indicating I was not a human in this memory). All the people there just looked up at me and seemed surprised at this outburst of speech. They were looking a bit taken aback but I was feeling quite amused at my surprise for them and I believe I was chuckling to myself. This to me was clearly my primary incarnation (PI) on a ship wherever that ship is. The dream switched and I remember fiddling about with some clothing I was either getting out of, or getting into, I am not exactly sure and then I was sitting in what seemed like a swimming pool (on reflection the clothes and pool could be a metaphor for getting into my human avatar in the immersion pod which may have fluid in it, this is just supposition though). I was at the corner of the pool and propping myself up with my arms over the edge of the pool looking into the pool area. Then I saw at the far end of the pool, off to my left, 4 or 5 ladies walking along towards the side which came up to where I was in the pool. Then one of the ladies walked up the side of the pool towards me, she came right up to where I was, she bent down and got her face really close to mine and whispered something to me. She was a Caucasian lady with long blonde hair pulled back in some loose braids tied at the back of her head, I remember her face very well and her lips, I think the lips stood out as I was watching them as she was speaking, which I guess is important as everyone is telepathic and to whisper something in voice must have been quite secret. I do not recall what she said however.

I was watching YouTube and saw a CA video with a picture of 'Alenym' on it, Alenym apparently is the present 'Queen' or head of the Taygetan Pleiadians, I immediately got the sense that this is who was whispering to me in the dream. The likeness was not as I remember her, and I believe that the CA channel have used actresses images that they portray as the 'real' Taygetans, but I got the feeling or 'knowing' that is who it was. Obviously with my apparent position in my race (I am not sure but maybe it spans different races of Pleiadians as I believe that I am a 'Blue pleiadian') and Alenym if indeed 'Alenym' is her genuine name (this is what CA say that it is) and the Taygetans are very human looking, together with my close friend Raani who is an ambassador for his race and attends Galactic federation meetings, means that perhaps it is not too out of the ordinary that Alenym would be speaking with me, and I think that the bunch of ladies that were present when I spoke Spanish were Alenym and her entourage. She does have protection such as bodyguards and aides, and they are apparently all or mostly ladies as well, if the CA information is to be believed. I felt 'different' after this dream and the whispering from Alenym, more confident, a bit happier with a different stride to my step. I talked with Ruth about this dream as it seemed important. Ruth tuned into the event and said she got the word 'Elohim' and that Alenym had unlocked something in me that was connected to this word. So I researched the Elohim and its possible relation to my PI and it seems that the Blue Pleiadians have a species connection to the Elohim and that the Elohim are kin to the Blue Pleiadians of 'Celeano' which is one of the stars in the Pleiades, they always refer to where they are from naming the star, but they live on one of the planets that are around that star. I got from the Mary Rodwell regression that I am from Aldebaran which is a star in the constellation Taurus, but I believe through Raani that my PI originated in Celeano but perhaps is presently living in Aldebaran. My PI who is from Celeano would then speak the 'Celeste' language, but also because they are kin to the Elohim have the 'Elohimieth' language. So it would be one of these languages that were probably on the immersion pods control keypad. The Elohim are from Asterope (apparently) and it is apparently the name connected to the Bible stories, so is therefore very loaded. The Andromedan species is very old with very few known variants, but one of them is also the Celestes or Blue Pleiadian. The Andromedan races apparently were similar to humans millions of years ago with a lack of ethics and morals and eventually destroyed their own planet (this is the story from CA). They have since got no planet of their own and have become completely space based, they have three classes of ships one is called 'the Grand sphere' which contains millions of inhabitants, and the Earth's terrestrial moon is apparently an example of one of their bioships as it was theirs originally. The Indian language of Sanskrit is apparently a humanisation of the Andromedan language. Their average height is 2.4meters, so very tall, and so I wonder if my PI and Blue Pleiadians have inherited a tall stature as well as a blue skin from the Andromedan's?

So, I then also assumed that Norri is a Blue Pleiadian, and through Ruth and using a pendulum that seems to be the case, so I attempted drawing her as she really looks, through a kind of automatic drawing, which is what happened when drawing My PI. I have asked Norri if she would appear to me as her true self, but she seems to be reluctant. I think she appears to me at the level of attractiveness, with which I see her when I am my PI, as she doesn't want me to be put off by her in what would seem to me as 'Trevor' as an 'alien' appearance. I am not bothered, but she has said not to worry as we find each other attractive where we are together, so I leave it with her as to whatever makes her comfortable.

March 27th 2022 – plus update September 2022 Dream, that's actually a memory – Not sure of the exact start, but it seemed that we, me and a couple of others, were in some sort of 'time loop', there was a super massive machine that I had in my mind was a 'world manipulator' and that it needed to be destroyed. People were running away, taking stuff with them that they thought they wanted, looting in other words as it all seemed to be coming down. Some of the 'people' were still there and they were torturing someone, and that we were there to rescue him. He was lying face down on a metal table, naked with his hands and feet tied down so he could not move. There were these huge needles on the ends of metal robotic arms and they were injecting him in many places on his back. I just saw a bubble of skin that had swelled up to a large size after a needle had jabbed him, going down slowly causing him much pain. I heard one of the torturers say "he doesn't know the answers", but I felt he did, but that he was strong enough to not give in, and was able to endure the pain of torture. The next thing I know is that we were looking for the 'control centre' and were climbing high up in a building to get there. Once there we contacted the extraction team to get extracted. A lady and her team had arrived to help us escape to the extraction point from this time loop place of world manipulation. I asked the lady what her name is, she was shorter than me, and I may have been a tall being? She had blond hair with black or darker shades of hair within her hair. She said her name to me and I tried to repeat her name, but I pronounced it not so well, so I tried again and this time I pronounced it very well, as I think she commented on it, it had a peculiar sound to me at the time. The first part of her name I will try to write down so as to give the correct English sound: Schkier –mach – derr, I have split it into 3 parts, the last two parts I am not 100% are accurate, but the first part is exactly right, it has stuck permanently in my brain.. It has a long 'shhh' sound at the beginning, which slides seamlessly into the next part with a sharp 'K' sound followed by an 'eeear' sound. I have spelt it how I perceive it to be spelt, after the

hyphen is the sound like 'mack' and after the next hyphen is the 'der' sound.
She then looked at me with surprise at my excellent pronunciation of her name. Then she said "I thought you might like to know your name", and she said it is "Wulf-en-deer" again the first part is exactly as she said it I have spelt it how I think it should be spelt, and it was pronounced 'oolf' – 'un' – 'deea'. So this is not the name that I believe at the moment is my 'Blue Pleiadian' name but maybe a name I went by as another different being as another avatar perhaps on a different mission? I really don't know, maybe it is my PI name? That was the end of the dream. After this experience I was using the Google language translation on my browser and getting different languages to say certain words, I found the Dutch *(although on another recent attempt it was Afrikaans language,* **West Germanic language of South Africa,** *developed from* **17th-century Dutch,** *sometimes called Netherlandic)* pronunciation to be almost exactly as I heard the lady say our names in this memory, interesting. Then a few months later I started to watch a movie on Netflix called "The forgotten battle" As I watched the opening few moments when people were speaking I saw there were subtitles in English along the bottom of the screen, I felt a little annoyed as they were speaking English, so why are there subtitles? Then the lady moved to another room and spoke to someone else, and they were speaking Dutch, I was quite confused as to why, I thought they spoke English first, why change to Dutch now? I reversed the movie back to the opening scene just to double-check only they were talking Dutch and not English? And yet I understood what they were saying when I first listened to it! But now I don't understand the language. So this I think was a nod to the genuineness and reality of my memory, and to the research pointing to Dutch as the language. The second confirmation about this memory was when I was meditating and in meditation I played over in my mind the events of the memory, only this time I found it was a very emotional event, I felt very sad and was crying over my colleague that was being tortured, I knew this was real for sure in myself now after this emotional reaction, that can still surface if I think about it.

The torture scene   *The looting and fleeing scene*

Schkier - Mach – Derr

Saturday 7th May 2022 - Every Saturday I use to join a zoom group which is made up of members of a facebook page 'Echo whispers' ran by a lady called Tress. It starts at 7.30pm and goes on until everyone has gotten tired or has other things to do, as some of the group come from different parts of the world I usually got tired and came off by 10 or 10.30pm. On this particular Saturday I was feeling more awake and less tired than usual and was staying on later, it got to about midnight when one of the members, a lady called 'Salena' who is normally quite quiet, started to speak, there was only 4 of us still on at that time as the others had gone off. Salena then proceeded to say that when she joins the zoom group she sees things around people on the group, or gets images and information regarding certain people she sees on there. She then said she wanted to speak to me about images and information that she is receiving regarding myself, and that she was 'prompted' to buy some paper and pens/pencils to draw images etc regarding the group. She proceeded to tell me what she was seeing and feeling, it was fascinating, so I asked her if she would send me pictures of her drawings and received information, and write down what she had told me, so I could keep it for myself and add to this collection of experiences I am writing. She has kindly done that and so I paste below the pictures and information she has given me over a few days whilst we have been in communication, with her blessing.

Hi Trevor, I have tried to put into words what I felt /saw whilst on several Echo Whispers zoom chats. I had been prompted for a few weeks prior to purchase a sketch pad and some pencils and to draw what I was seeing, whether physically or in my mind's eye. I have attached several drawings/ scribblings that I have done during a couple of the meetings, with a few wee bits being added in later, as I find when I think about what I've have been shown it leads to other things. There is one picture that is purely in relation to what I was picking up/being shown around / to do with you. I did mention that I was being pulled to do this and at the time everyone seemed ok by it, but on hindsight I should have properly asked everyone for permission, However I guess though if I wasn't supposed to see/feel it I wouldn't have.

It would be about a few weeks ago during a zoom meeting (I wish I dated these doodles now).. You were sitting quietly and the other guys were in full chat/ debate about(I can't even remember what they were talking about now to be honest) however my attention kept being drawn to you. And I clearly in my mind's eye saw you/but it wasn't you as you are now. But yet I knew it was you, if that make sense, Your were standing at one side of a set of 3 stone discs, these were stacked on top of each other, large, medium, small, all had markings carved into them, each disc different. On top of the smallest disc sat a large metallic bowl, which was filled with what looked like shimmering water that had a luminosity to it. At the other side were two more beings kneeling in respect. You were tall and had a light bluish skin with long (passed the shoulder) white/silvery hair. I couldn't really make out too much of the features, the beings kneeling looked similar from the back, they had some kind of long garment on (it could have been a cloak or similar as I was seeing the view from the back. the surroundings were very bright and made me think of rainforests even though I could not see the detail

at that time. it felt full of life, full of energy. There was an overwhelming feeling of importance to what was going on but also of acknowledgement for what you have done/achieved so far. It was a ceremony, of that I have no doubt. Even though I did not see them do it I knew what was in the bowl was for you. For your being which then led me to think about the significance of the water/ liquid in the bowl. This was an integration of you back to you, if that makes sense, it was a cleansing and merging of energy. I did feel overwhelmed to say to you as it felt it was and is important for you to know that your efforts are known and are fully appreciated(sorry if that's not the exact words) I'm just trying to convey the sentiment. I am sorry to say that at the time I lacked the confidence to say what I saw and that it did not come out until this Saturday, Which is strange as I truly believe everyone that left the chat earlier were meant to , to afford me the opportunity to speak to you. As again I was drawn to the significance of the work you are doing and that it was important to let you know. After we came off the chat, I always question what I've said etc, sometimes it prompts me to write down or draw other things. When I think of the ceremony I was aware that there were 3 moons/stars or planets in alignment from my viewing point. The first being large and red in colour, so I put that down along with the 3 in alignment with a few other scribblings. The following day whilst having a wash I was still pondering the significance of the water/liquid in the bowl, when clear as day the word ARCTURUS popped into my head. I later googled it to find it is actually a giant red star that is far more luminous than our sun (see scribblings on drawing). Arcturian/os also translates to Guardian/Watcher... which if I'm honest I was stunned at as I had drawn a large red planet/moon .
So again off I went with more information filtering through, I saw you (as you are now) lying in what looked like an oval open pod/type structure. It looked like it was made of a matt rock crystal or similar material. This was filled with the same liquid as in the bowl. It felt like you were asleep but not if that makes sense, as I felt the being that is you was there even though I did not see him. It reminded me of a floatation pod if that makes sense. I drew a rough picture of the face I had the impression of. (please excuse my poor artistic abilities) Picasso I am not. I have to stress the overwhelming feeling of importance of water/this liquid, and that if you have not tried this already, to submerse yourself in water (not over your head and connect) as it really feels like

lightening going off.. Last but not least I saw a energetic trail that leads from you to you.. it connects through time/space and dimensions, As it is all there all the answers you are looking for or more of what you have already found. Thank you for taking the time to read this Trevor and I hope some it if any makes sense to you. I have attached the scribblings I have done over several weeks of the chat including 1 page that is specifically for you. I cannot stress how appreciative I am for you allowing me to share with you what I experienced. I literally just write down what I see or feel and then later try and get some kind of confirmation/evidence. I do get it wrong so I am in no way saying I am 100% correct but I do need to trust myself more, so thank you for affording me that opportunity. As this is way out of my comfort zone as over the years I have kept it all just logged in journals. Thank you Have a great day Salena ps. something that did pop up was the experimental belief in proto matter. (Which is a liquid/water type substance which if given form is the alleged substance the universe is created from). I think I scribbled it down on one of the pages. Once I have sent this I can now read your PDF. Thank you so much for sharing it with me and I look forward to reading about your experiences.

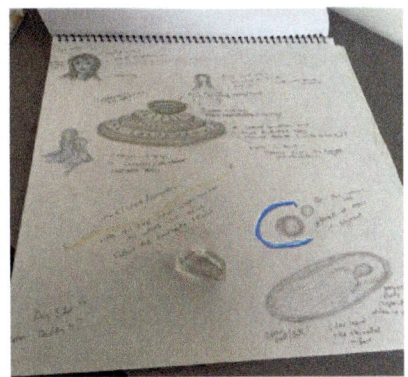 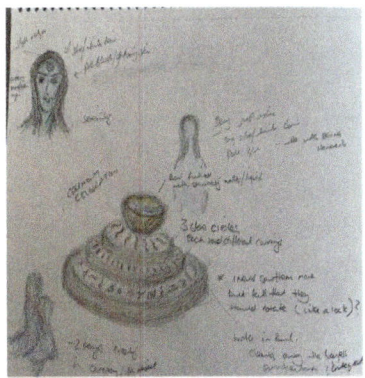

Salena's drawings

So I was amazed, my mind blown! Salena did not know of all the things about the immersion pod, my possible status in my race, the kind of being I am, anything. I showed Ruth the pictures and she said the other two beings kneeling on one side of the stone circles were Norri and my daughter, she felt the slight sadness but also the knowledge that I was doing something important, she saw that even the slightly taller figure had her arm around the shorter one being Nirri my daughter. I did not see this, but Ruth could feel it all from the picture. Also Ruth said she thought it was when I was leaving to come here, hence the sadness. The energetic trail I believe is the Portal and tunnel with the line of linked bubbles going through that I experienced. I will be meditating on that in the future, trying to make more connections and understanding. The stone circles reminded me of a stargate, and Salena has added that she saw them turning and opening up, so that seems to fit. The Pleiadians through Cosmic Agency have said that an amniotic type fluid is used in long term immersion pod usage, which fit with this special fluid that Salena had seen.

I am keeping in touch with Salena and there may be more information to come in the future. I feel very privileged to have got such great friends in helping me along my path of awakening and understanding and I hope I help them as much in return.

A few questions answered by Salena

Hi Salena, just looking at your drawing and trying to read your writing. Just a few questions 1) for the skin you put pale blue /glittery skin, is glittery right? Just interesting as when I first saw myself I looked silver, glittery could describe the kind of silver, although we know I am blue. 2) What did you write for my eyes I can't make it out? 3) On my forehead you drew and wrote 'something' ridges? is that right, what was the first word, I have tried to draw myself a few times, the first one I did draw some lines on my brow, so that makes sense 4) There's a word on the bottom right, is that 'serenity'? And lastly 5) The two beings that I believe is Norri and Niri, do they have the same coloured hair as me?

Salena
Hi Trevor I hope you are well. Of course.
- *The skin was blue however had a silvery shimmer. I've put glitter but what I meant was it has a glow a sheen to it that made it have a different dimension other worldly if that makes sense.*

- *The eyes were the most beautiful blue colour like water. But again that could be how it was shown to me. They were very peaceful almost hypnotic. I know this may sound strange but when you lose all resistance to everything and find peace. I hope that makes sense.*

- *Yes it was ridges, just slight the impression I got when doing it was that it denoted position. The more ridges the higher up the, I won't use the word rank as I feel that would be wrong but more evolved/wise would be a better way of describing the feeling.*

- *When doing the drawing I believe the two beings are Norri & Nirri did have the same hair colour. But that could just be how it was shown so I knew you were all together.*

You're very welcome. Fantastic you are looking for more answers and information which I'm sure will follow. Sometimes I think a shower is just as good as a bath. One things for sure if you have to be in a bath or floatarium then somehow that will come about. Have a fantastic day. ps Sorry my handwriting is so scribbly. I tend to write quickly.

Norri as I believe she really looks like

October 2022 – Dream state at night, I believe it was probably my PI rather than another incarnation, but, I can't be sure. I was in a room, I think there were windows in front of me along the wall, and it seemed quite bright in this room. In front of me was a being. This being was a lot shorter than myself, I was looking down on 'her' I just 'knew' she was a female. She had a grey face, and around the edges of her face that I think continued further around the head, I don't know about the body, that was a dark blue colour, and it was all very short dense fur. I then looked away from her face to the left, the wall on the left was white. I heard her say, "There's no need to look away". I apologised and said "sorry, force of habit" (I don't know why this is a force of habit) so I turned my head back to face her again, I saw more detail of the face, I then turned my head away again but to the right side, again the wall to the right was white. I laughed at myself and said "sorry" and turned my head back to look at her face. This time her face was perfectly clear and I saw her eyes, she had absolutely massive bright yellow eyes, like cats eyes, and even her face was reminiscent of a cat's, but not exactly like a cat, and I couldn't see the ears like a cat has, in fact I couldn't see any ears at all. She might have had ear canals on the side of her head, but I didn't see around the head so I don't know. And then whilst looking into those massive yellow eyes, I just said in my mind "what a beautiful being" as this was the overwhelming feeling I was having whilst looking at her. I felt these words were not 'mine' as the observer of the event, but were the thoughts of the person living the experience at the actual time it was happening in the past, as I felt this was a memory. Looking at her face with those eyes, reminded me very much of one of my cats 'Bella' when she looks up at me. I drew a picture below of her it's a poor rendition but gives you the general idea of she looks.

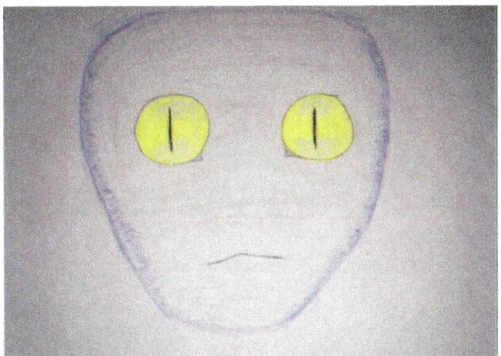

Cat-like being, I don't recall a nose either

October 2022 – Meeting with Kai update I was feeling 'encouraged' to do a drawing of the meeting with my PI event. So I put pencil to paper and started drawing the whole event in a one page 'snapshot' which is below. I didn't really know or understand 'why' I was to do this, but there was a 'feeling' in the back of mind it would help me to understand it better. I showed Ruth this picture, and she said she gets the part which is 'Trevor' and the part which is my PI, but she was getting 'nothing' from the area I travelled to, in which my PI appears to me. As soon as she said that, I realised what was going on.
Trevor IS my Primary Incarnation, and my Primary Incarnation IS Trevor, my experience with falling through the bed and being instantly in my body in the pod as my primary incarnation with absolutely NO delay or time spent travelling made me connect that with meeting my PI. The whole portal event, with travelling through the portal to the 'event space' where I came out, and seeing 'other' people, was nothing but a mental construct created by my primary incarnation to ease me, 'Trevor', into the idea of 'going' somewhere and meeting my PI, my other higher self. Ruth felt 'nothing' because it didn't exist except as a mental construct. I think it was the best way to get me to start to understand that I am not just 'Trevor' here, but also someone else with a whole other, different life. My PI could just pop into my head, but that would have been too jarring, suddenly a voice and 'alien' face claiming to be me would have been an even harder pill to swallow, and maybe would have made me think I was losing it, or being manipulated by an unknown outside force. As indeed my PI IS me, HE/I knew what was the

best approach to start this new deeper level of understanding, revealing an even deeper layer to my reality and to begin the connection process.

Meeting with my primary incarnation

My analogy on the Multiversality of our existence

We are beings of 10 frequencies, the physical part of us residing in the first 3 frequencies, but I want you to imagine that you are a first frequency level being (one dimensional in old currency) literally a dot on a piece of A4 paper. The physical environment in which you live is the 2nd frequency environment (2nd dimension in old money) length and breadth, and the thickness of the paper and the surrounding environment etc is the 3rd frequency (or time dimension in old money) you move forwards in your life as a 1st frequency being along a line on the paper surface which is your physical environment, and the movement forwards is through the 3rd frequency or what we think of as 'time'. You can only go forwards in 'time' just like us, so you are travelling along this line in a forward direction. Now imagine someone pushes a pencil through the paper, right through the 'life line' of your 1st frequency self. The 'life line' would have to go around the pencil, so as you hit the pencil, it essentially is 'blocking' your life, you would 'hit' the pencil, but not understand 'what' it is but you would only know that 'something' is blocking your life, and that you would have to go in another direction either this way, or that way, to get around this block.

So this 1st frequency being lives in this 3rd frequency environment, he cannot see, smell, taste or touch this 3rd frequency it is only that he moves through it. In the same way as we as the physical 3rd frequency beings move through 'time' but we cannot see, smell, taste or touch it, but we move through it in one direction. Let's say that this 1st frequency being manages, through, let's say meditation, to get their consciousness to let go of the 1st frequency body and come into the 3rd frequency environment, and as he does this he manages to 'see' this pencil. Now he would not understand 'what' this pencil is, what its use is or anything, he cannot really fully comprehend it. But he can see that it is there 'blocking' his life and therefore he has to go around it. Because his life is only 1st frequency he would only have some kind of distorted view of this pencil, he might see some colours or some shapes, but he will not be able to comprehend it fully, he will have no words or language to describe it, but he will simply 'see' in some way that there is 'something' that is the block in his life.

So when he goes back into his 1st frequency body, he might try to explain what he experienced to others. They will likely think him 'weird', 'strange' or off his head, because he will not be able to explain it properly, he would say 'there are these things blocking our lives' and they exist on another plane of existence, some will think he is a liar or mad or just trying to get attention.

This 1st frequency being is living in his life, in a line, on this 2nd frequency plane of existence, he cannot see the edges of the paper, or the depth of the paper, the 3rd frequency. So this paper with his life on it is 'a whole'. So we, as 3rd frequency beings can see his life as a whole, we can see the life line, and the start of his life and the end of his life, as we are looking 'down' onto this lower frequency level plane of existence. We can interact with him at any point on his 'life' because we have access to the whole from our vantage point. We could even place that pencil through his life line. He has no idea of the true purpose or reason of this pencil, that it is an implement, a tool, which we use to draw, or to write for communication. Let alone would he have the concept of these absolutely massive (from his perspective) beings that use these tools. Just think of the size of this 1st frequency being, and the size of us, third frequency beings, we are millions of times the size of this dot on a piece of paper. He cannot possibly imagine it or grasp the concept of us, and that we put the pencil through his life line. Or that we live in the 3rd frequency in our own time space, and have chairs, tables on which his whole environment sits, or houses, cars, country. He would never be able to grasp the enormity or meaning of it all, it is completely outside his vision, imagination, understanding or concept, there is no way with him being just a point on a piece of paper.

Now his life on the 2nd frequency plane of existence is complicated and full of rich detail in his opinion, but from our perspective his life is very plain compared to ours, not even to mention other planets and the universe as we understand it. So the difference in size and complexity from this 2nd frequency life to our 3rd frequency life and understanding is almost immeasurable and totally incomprehensible from his perspective.

Now as you see the difference in complexity from the 2nd to 3rd frequency, you can see the parallel I am drawing for us in the 3rd frequency in comparison to the 4th, 5th up to 12th frequency levels. Then onto the 2nd dimension and the first frequency level in the first sub component of the 2nd dimension, where that is a whole new universe and the size and complexity is x12 from this first dimension, and there are hundreds more universes above that. I think you can start to see the enormity and complexity of it all.

Now just think of the physics which these 1st frequency beings use as tools in their environment, for them these are useful tools and help them to live and prosper in their own plane of existence. But from our perspective, these tools are child's toys, they are useful for them, but not at all useful to us, we have a much more complex understanding of reality and have the tools which reflect that understanding. So you can imagine that there is a much greater understanding in the higher frequency realms on those planes of existence compared to our own. So it could be that when we look at quantum physics for example, all the known physics and tools we use in our macro environment are no longer valid and break down. Perhaps that is because we are getting a glimpse of a higher frequency plane of existence.

Let's take this analogy a bit further as 3rd frequency beings perhaps we want to take a look at this 1st frequency being and his life and environment in the 2nd frequency. So we develop a tool with which we can view their lives and how they live in their realm of existence. We can then come in and view them at any point in their lives and any life in particular, as we see them all as lines on a sheet of paper. We might even want to experience what it is like to be a 1st frequency being living in a very restricted life, in view and understanding, see how it feels, what troubles and strife they experience, the joys and happiness. This would be for scientific and perhaps even for our own interest to go through their frustrations and experiences they have in order to add to our own understanding, for evolutionary and spiritual progression. We would develop a way of making a dot on this plane of existence or of using a dot already there and downloading a small part of our consciousness into this dot in order to live there, for the extent of the life of that 1st frequency being. We live outside of that 'time frame' of these 1st frequency beings, and so when that life is finished, we simply come back to our body in our own plane of existence and hardly, if any, 'time' has passed for us in our own 3rd frequency existence.

I am sure you can see the parallel I am making here with my own experience of being a secondary incarnation on this planet in this plane of existence. And indeed of being an aspect of a TES which is outside of any 'time frame' that we can possibly imagine.

I just want to add that the consciousness and understanding that we have is always limited by the plane of existence in which we are living, like an internet speed. The lower the frequency plane we live on lowers the bandwidth of our consciousness and understanding, so as a 3rd frequency being we are running on a 512mb/s (or lower) bandwidth, as opposed to the 12k mb/s on a 4th frequency perhaps, but I think the difference is probably greater than we can imagine.

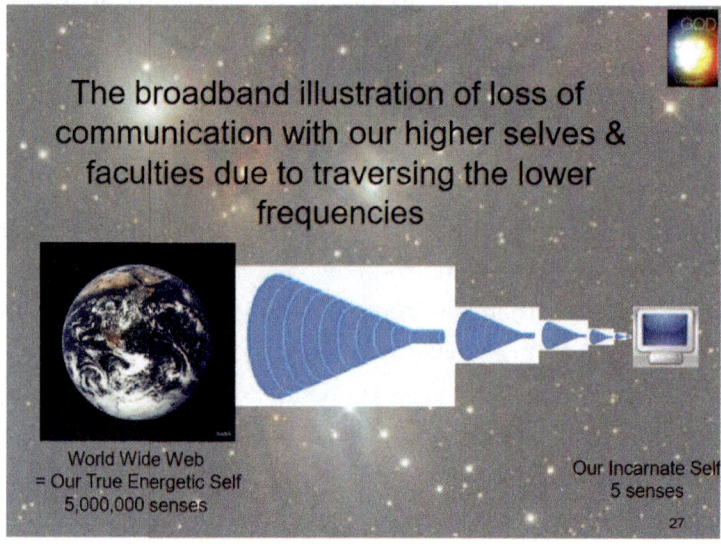

Guy's illustration of this loss of bandwidth

(A 'beyond the source production'.copyright © Guy Steven Needler. All rights reserved

So we cannot grasp fully our place here in the hierarchy of sentient conscious beings throughout the multiverse, we can only see things from our own perspective from our level of plane of existence. But we are all much higher sentient beings living in all the levels of the multiverse right back to the source and the origin. It is possible to connect with our higher selves and raise our frequency through spiritual practices like meditation to move forwards in our spiritual evolution and understanding, and that is the purpose of our lives here in this the lowest dimension of the multiverse, to learn and evolve and to eventually become sources ourselves. You are Multiversal.

Further Reading

Guy Steven Needler

http://www.beyondthesource.org/

Link to guys books on Amazon:

https://www.amazon.co.uk/stores/Guy-Steven-Needler/author/B005EYSBTO?ref=ap_rdr&store_ref=ap_rdr&isDramIntegrated=true&shoppingPortalEnabled=true

Aldous Huxely - perennial philosophy

Eknath Easwaran – The Upanishads

Plato – republics

https://www.youtube.com/@CosmicAgency

Printed in Great Britain
by Amazon